A Thundering Silence

A Thundering Silence

Nannette Morrison

cover photo:
Irish Brigade Monument at Gettysburg, by Barbara Doeinck

Manufactured in the United States of America

ISBN 1-880404-10-9

Designed and produced by BOOKWRIGHTS of Charlottesville
2522 Willard Drive
Charlottesville, VA 22903
804-296-0686

To purchase additional copies of this book contact:
Nannette Morrison
1310 Lester Drive
Charlottesville, VA 22901
804-293-9650

Contents

Contents

A Thundering Silence

Introduction

There are so many things to know, so many avenues to explore. It is the intelligent and courageous mind who ignores the dogma of old patterns and fear handed on to us from past generations. Truly the Spiritual Seeker has the trust in his faith to learn Truth, Honesty, and Wisdom, then to live these virtues daily.

I wish to honor the people who have come forward with their experiences since the writing of *Echoes of Valor*. Herein *A Thundering Silence* are recorded only a minute sampling of the lives now learning the 'other side' of true spirituality.

The questions raised by such high numbers of people witnessing these energy forms, as well as literally being contacted by the 'dead,' are quite straightforward. People are seeking the truth in these phenomena. No longer are they content to have them swept under the carpet, to be ignored, nor to be categorized as 'delusions.'

Volumes of speculations are already written on the explanations of ghosts, angels, and other contacts from the spiritual realms. A high degree of these seem to conflict with each other. However, it is important to realize that numerous possibilities exist simultaneously. Energy thought-forms can be suspended in space to appear once again to the highly sensitive individual. Particularly emotional or traumatic events can produce very dramatic results hundreds of years beyond the time-frame of their original occurrence.

These possibilities do not explain, however, the direct contact by an entity directed to living individuals still on the earth plane. One cannot discard conscious communication between us and the spiritual realms when individuals are being given specific details such as names, dates, and events. In numerous instances these 'forgotten' spirits are begging for help. We now are beginning to realize that through the vehicles of several religions world-wide, it is possible to assist these entities on their rightful journeys.

Through the auspices of Christianity, angels may appear to us in many forms, as may the Christ Consciousness. Proof is abundant that Satan is also alive and well in the world today. He too is quite efficient at manifesting spirits, using deception and trickery to allure the unsuspecting mind.

Tibetan teachings explain the stages of dying and the choices which must be made as the deceased reaches for the Clear Light. These stages (Bardos) can last several days or longer while the subject remains in confusion as to his status. The 'soul complex' emerges from its experience of the Void into a state somewhat like a dream.

An infinity of worlds exist simultaneously, all operating at different frequencies. On the higher levels of vibrations, is a timeless zone. These higher levels are interacting with our physical ones all the time. We all occupy the same space but on different wave frequencies. Consequently, it is feasible that the various levels of activities co-exist with a minimal amount of conscious interaction. This also makes it possible for an astral traveler to perceive what appears as solid matter, as well as artifacts common to the physical world.*

I encourage the reader to explore beyond the physical world of matter, to believe in life after 'death.' Such knowledge can enrich our understanding of everyday events which frequently seem to be beyond our control.

A few of the situations recorded herein seem to differ from the manner in which history records them. I believe that accuracy lies in the first-hand account, as opposed to how the story is retold.

---

*These opinions are my own and do not necessarily reflect those of the institutions or organizations mentioned in the text.

'Thou shalt understand that it is a science most profitable, and passing all other sciences, for to learn to die. For a man to know that he shall die, that is common to all men; as much as there is no man that may ever live or he hath hope or trust thereof; but thou shalt find full few that have this cunning to learn to die... I shall give thee the mystery of this doctrine; the which shall profit thee greatly to the beginning of ghostly health, and to a stable fundament of all virtues.'—*Orologium Sapientiae.*

'Against his will he dieth that hath not learned to die. Learn to die and thou shalt learn to live, for there shall none learn to live that hath not learned to die.'—Toure of all Toures: and Teacheth a Man for to Die.
(from *The Book of the Craft of Dying*)

Memories of War

"Do you believe in strange things happening sometimes?" Warren addressed the question tentatively,

Bill responded carefully, weighing his words, "Well, I'm not sure. But what do you mean?"

The Georgia reenactment unit was sitting around an evening campfire. Most of them were sharing personal experiences, not only about the Civil War, but including firsthand battle encounters. Warren, a Vietnam veteran, needed to share this experience with his comrades. "Well, I'm convinced of it," he continued. "Let me tell you what happened in Vietnam. Now, most soldiers believe that when it's your time to go, it's your time to go. Whether you want to or not doesn't matter."

"Yeah, I guess so," agreed Bill who was beginning to think it over more carefully. He had been in service in Korea, Germany, and the Middle East, but not a tour of duty in Vietnam.

"I was at Hamburger Hill," the senior sergeant went on. "We lost an awful lot of guys trying to take that hill. The North Vietnamese were very well entrenched on the hill. We took a tremendous number of casualties, percentage-wise; the units that went up the hill just got it in the shorts! The things we saw that day are the things of which horror movies are made."

Warren shook his head at the morose memories. "The hill was quite steep, and all the trees had been blasted off it. The Americans would assault the hill and get thrown back down. Then they would stand back, hit it with napalm, artillery, and air strikes. Again, they'd start back up the hill and get thrown back down. The scene was awful! I recall moving what I thought was a burning tree limb. But

6

as soon as I touched it, I realized it was a man's leg that had been blown off—really nasty stuff!

"So, after the Americans finally took Hamburger Hill, we put a perimeter out even though we were exhausted. All around lay hundreds and hundreds of bodies of soldiers from both sides. But it was getting dark, and we were afraid of a counterattack. Suddenly, one of my guys started firing! We called for flares. Everybody ran to their posts, preparing for what might be a counterattack."

Warren stared directly at Bill. "I will swear an oath to what I saw next. I know then that I saw the Grim Reaper! It was the huge, black form of a human with his back to me. He would run over to a soldier who'd fallen, bend over him, touch him, then cackle in a horrible loud laugh. The shape would stand up, walk over to another man and do the same to him.

"You know, we tried at first to attribute the scene to battle fatigue. But every single guy in my company saw exactly the same thing! The men were shooting at it, but all their bullets passed through it. I still picture our tracers going through this huge, ugly body and coming out the other side. Then when this thing got pretty close to me; it turned toward me and looked directly at me! It was laughing in a sickening way. I was staring at the white face of a skull with empty, black, eye sockets. Suddenly, it vanished." Warren paused in his conversation.

Bill felt a heaviness as he considered all this. He knew Warren to be a man of extensive military experience and certainly a reliable, down-to-earth guy. Bill listened further while Warren spoke. "I did three tours in Vietnam; believe me when I say I had lots of battle exposure. But this experience with the Grim Reaper at Hamburger Hill was what truly bothered me the most. Every single body that had been touched by this thing died afterward. Our men were totally unprepared for the whole experience. They thought at first that someone was out there stripping the dead. They were infuriated at that idea after everything they'd endured in the fighting. That was why all their weapons were focused on this single figure! It took a short while for each one to realize that these weapons weren't having any effect whatsoever on this form. To witness those tracers passing through the figure and meeting a mark beyond it was devastating to them."

Other similar occurrences have been reported from various wars. A few Civil War reenactors participating in Gettysburg reenactments reportedly have had similar experiences. Usually, the effect is so startling that they are reluctant to discuss it.

Then in Vietnam, the villagers have set aside a special day in which they visit the battle-torn areas to "feed the ghosts" of soldiers who have fought and died there. Do we not in our own country, as well as in Europe, celebrate Halloween or All Saint's Day?

Nevertheless, the four of us who visited Cold Harbor Battlefield one afternoon in July, 1994 are wondering if we too didn't come nearly face-to-face with the Grim Reaper. One Reenactor of the 19th Virginia. Infantry Regiment and Tim Fredrickson of the 5th Virginia. Infantry Regiment were walking toward the Union trenches. My mother, Carolyn Morrison, and I stood at the edge of the Confederate trenches. A large flash of black darted across my field of vision, crossing the battle area in front of the Union trenches. The size of it startled me, but I reasoned that I had only seen a bird flying behind the distant tree line.

Carolyn saw it too. She described it as remarkable in size for a crow or buzzard. But it was a flowing, black movement which disappeared behind a tree. Neither of us were to see it come out from behind the tree.

After photographing the area of the Confederate perspective, we joined Tim and Sam around the Union side. Still, we did not mention our experience with the dark form. The two men walked among the trees toward Federal embankments. Suddenly, the vile odor of rotting human flesh, accompanied by gunpowder, attacked the nostrils! Both men came rushing out of the area; both were gagging, spitting and nearly sick from the stench.

Because of Tim's combat duty with Desert Storm, he was more certain of the smells he was identifying. Yet, each of the two would take several minutes to recover from the event. Both felt a distinct sense of dread before they had entered that exact spot.

Seeing their reactions, Carolyn and I walked in toward the location of the smells. Although neither of us was familiar with the odor of human flesh in decay, we too became aware of the awful smell. Yet, there was nothing physically visible as the source. What remained was the feeling of such a mournful waste of young lives.

The Martha

The apparition floated a foot above the floor. She wore the long, white nurse's dress typical of those worn by the Martha girls during the Civil War, as well as the high-topped boots of the era. From the closed doorway of the ballroom and down the hall outside the gift shop, passed this figure of the young woman. She was walking directly toward the late night security camera. Was this spirit, rumored by hotel personnel to have been captured on film late in 1994, that of Beth?

She was a first year student at Martha Washington College when the Civil War erupted. Although most of the students returned home at the outbreak of war, several remained to nurse wounded soldiers. Beth was one who had chosen to stay.

Captain John Toves was a Yankee soldier left in Abingdon to spy on activities of Confederate troops. He was discovered while hiding behind a tree near the courthouse. Captain Toves was shot several times in the abdomen. At his capture, he was dropped onto the college lawns. Nurses ran out and carried the man, screaming in pain, up the steps and into what is now room 403. The Yankee's blood dripped all the way up the fourth floor stairway. The young inexperienced nurse Beth was assigned to care for him.

"My pain is terrible! Please help me!" Captain Toves cried.

His yelling made Beth distraught. She grabbed her petticoat hem and tore it off hastily to make a bandage for the soldier. For many weeks she stayed by his side. His bleeding increased and a high fever set in. Beth fell in love with the man—a love which he returned. Still, he became weaker, then delirious.

Near midnight of his final evening, John Toves suddenly mustered up what bit of strength remained. He attempted to raise himself on one elbow, but fell back in agony. He begged his beloved, "Play...something...Beth. I'm going...the pain is...so terrible."

She was startled and trembling. She was at a loss for what to do to save him. Beth began playing the violin and singing a sweet, southern melody, one of the many she'd played to soothe him through his illness. Through mournful tears, she played the last notes and watched the life leave the man she loved so dearly.

The girl was devastated by Captain Toves' death. In her grief, Beth took ill with scarlet fever. It was Captain John's name that she called as she died. Beth begged for the other nurses to sing that same sweet, southern melody which she had sung for her Yankee lover. Later, she would be buried near him in the old Sinking Springs Cemetery.

For many years after her death, the Martha girls could hear Beth playing those mournful tones of the violin. They, as well as others, believed that the ghost of Beth returned to that room where Captain Toves died.

Such is only one of the stories of the famous Martha Washington Inn, a four star hotel and grand lady so rich with history. Built in 1832 and named Preston Hall by General Francis Preston, it became his home and that of his wife, Sarah Buchanon Campbell, and their nine children. Sarah's mother, Elizabeth Henry Campbell, was a sister to Patrick Henry.

Preston Hall was quite a lavish home, entertaining many famous travelers. General Preston, once a congressman, enjoyed the company of various politicians and influential figures. It remained their residence until after the death of Mrs. Francis Preston on July 23, 1846 when she passed away in the master bedroom downstairs. The glorious home sat vacant for some time.

A school for women was established on July 4, 1854. Building was well underway in 1855. However, that winter a heavy snow caused the new tin roof to collapse, resulting in considerable damage. The entire building project was abandoned. By 1858 the Martha Washington College project was rescued by the Holston Conference of the Methodist Church. Preston Hall became Martha Washington College in 1859 when it was purchased by the Holston Conference.

March 5, 1860 the school's first session began. It operated continuously through that year. When the war began in 1861, the college immediately felt the effects. It was on these lawns that John Mosby, later known as the "Gray Ghost," received much of his cavalry training. A member of the Washington County Mounted Rifles, commanded by Captain William E. "Grumble" Jones, John Mosby successfully raided Northern Virginia. Thus the name "Mosby's Confederacy" was adopted for the areas surrounding Abingdon.

Even into 1863 Martha Washington College prospered and grew. Yet, Confederate troops moved into the vicinity, using its grounds for training. Further Yankee attacks became disruptive and unsettling, making studies increasingly difficult. The college served more as a hospital to both Confederates and Yankees as the Civil War continued.

In the midst of the skirmishes, some fifteen or so Confederate boys who were friends of the Martha nurses hid in the old gymnasium (today the President's Club). The tunnels and secret passageways which begin there, permitted them to sneak under the floors and between the walls. One of these soldiers was carrying important papers describing the strength and location of Union troops. These were to be delivered eastward to General Robert E. Lee. This courier was in love with one of the Martha girls and wished to say "good-bye" before such a dangerous mission. Accompanied by his comrades, the young soldier slipped through the trap door presently located in the wall beside the marble bust on the second floor landing.

Yankee troops suddenly burst through the front door. A heated gun battle erupted on the stairs. Seven men were shot; five of these quickly died in the arms of the Martha girls. Such was the fate of the courier. Attempting to defend himself, he was shot down in front of his sweetheart. His blood stained the floor at her feet. Blood from the gunfight dripped down the beautiful spiral staircase.

Although most of the legends of the Martha Washington Inn have been recorded and passed down through history, the stories of current activities seem very much alive. Pete Sheffey, employed there since 1950, conducts tours and vividly recounts his own experiences, as well as other's. "My grandfather Wiley Henry worked here from 1890 to 1967. His job at night was to go around from hallway to hallway carrying a clock, punching all the clocks on each floor. There were no lights, only lanterns. So he carried a gas lantern around with him. He told me that many nights he would pass ghosts of soldiers in these halls. One night my grandfather walked up on a Confederate soldier crossing the hall. Grandfather offered to help him with a door before he realized who he was talking to. He was almost touching it before he ran away scared toward the fire escape."

As I met Pete for a two-hour tour of the Martha, he described her in a manner displaying his pride at being a part of her life and history. "The front lobby was the college library, but originally was the Preston family's living room. Most of the antiques you see here, as well as in the front hallway, are original from the college days."

I stood admiring the spaciousness of the rooms and high ceilings. It was early December. The Christmas tree and decorations were all around. A gas fire was lit in the fireplace. A visitor couldn't resist experiencing the quaintness and nostalgia of a winter in 1863. If I shifted my gaze toward the winding staircase, I could picture the Martha girls descending in colonial ball gowns. This was reminiscent of an annual elegant reception to honor President Washington. Once in the stately parlors, they would dance the minuet and the Virginia reel, escorted by dashing soldier lovers.

Pete's voice reminded me it was 1994. "Back in 1884 during renovation of the hotel, many of the pictures of Martha girls were hung. These are the ones you'll find on the hall walls. These other downstairs rooms were parlors used for greeting dates and were also used for conferences. Now, below us is the present day pub. But years ago it was the slave quarters. Our ghosts really like it down there, especially at night after the bar is closed."

We walked toward the enchanting Colonial staircase. "This upstairs floor is really haunted," declared Pete as we climbed upward. "I had an experience in the Virginia Suite about five weeks ago. I was trying to get in one of its room for a television remote control. Only, it seemed as though someone was inside the room holding the door shut!" he exclaimed in earnest. "I pushed and leaned with my whole weight before it opened. Suddenly, it opened real easily! Believe me, it wasn't like it was stuck; the door just flew open with no one inside!" What impressed Pete next was the unusual sensation of pressure inside the room. "The energy seemed like someone was pressing against my face, really warm," he described. "All I could think of to say was 'God loves you, Beth! God loves you.' I felt as though I was being pushed across the room. As I got to the TV and reached out my hand for the remote, it flew wildly off the TV and onto the floor before I could grab it! Finally, I picked it up and got out into the hall. That was the end of it. I haven't experienced anything in the spot since."

Once on the third floor landing, the Governor's Suite was to our right. Pete unlocked the door, allowing me to enter the spacious and opulent room. The suite was breathtaking. "There are unusual things that will happen in here," Pete resumed his story. "The gas logs in these fireplaces will go out spontaneously. The gas company comes in every so often to check out the mechanisms, but they can't find any problems with them. It's just like somebody up here doesn't want them to burn!"

We left the Governor's Suite to approach the Napoleon Room. I had to admire the grandfather clock standing so stately in the hallway. Upon entering the adjacent room, an immediate energy overlay recorded over our taped conversation. So much so, that no matter how loudly I played the tape, Pete's voice was blocked by static and humming. Nevertheless, after we gradually walked away from the center of the room toward the door, I was able to decipher Pete's words. "Many people have seen a ghost or heavy white energy film leave this area of the room and float upward, disappearing into the heater duct over the Napoleon bed. One guest woke up one night to see a soldier standing there at the foot of the bed watching him sleep.

"Let's go over here across the hall, and I'll show you the Johnson Suite, the other master bedroom of the Preston Family. This is where the dumbwaiters come up from downstairs and are located near the fireplace. President Woodrow Wilson's daughter attended Martha Washington College. While she was here, she used this suite to entertain many friends, as well as her cousins. Some of us feel that something traumatic happened in the Preston family that caused this room to be haunted," Pete speculated on the possibilities, such as a young child dying there. "All sorts of 'unexplainable' occurrences manifest here in Suite 300. Furniture gets rearranged when the room sits vacant, items fall on the floor, vapor or clouds of mist are witnessed, flashes of elusive images pass before the mirrors. Some of our maids have seen imprints of weight on the bed coverlets after they are freshly made up and smoothed out."

This suite remains the one of the most popular at the hotel. Its romantic beauty is irresistible.

Pete launched into more lore. "Last year, a gentleman stayed in the Johnson suite for six months during the winter. He absolutely fell in love with this room! Near the end of his visit late one evening, he came downstairs and commented to me, 'Pete, there's a ghost in my room. Strange things are happening up there.' He spoke quite freely to me about it. He said, 'I'll be in the shower and hear people talking in my room; but when I get out of the shower, they'll be gone! I'll be lying in bed at night watching TV when the bathroom spigots come on by themselves. One night I awoke to see a man standing over me. Pete, that happened eight or nine times!'"

The bell captain went on to describe his own experiences with the Johnson Suite, "I've felt a lot of pressure up here, lots of cold, then lots of heat. The fireplaces won't stay lit in here either. We have panel lights installed in these rooms, which can be raised or lowered. But, they come on and go off as they choose."

I looked around admiringly, feeling the ambiance to be warm and inviting. The circa 1850 sleigh bed is so unique. Then I encouraged Pete to continue with the legends of the Martha.

"Many bodies of the dead soldiers were stored in this bedroom before their burial. This was a temporary morgue for part of the war. One of the Confederate soldiers was shot in the back by a Yankee, near the courthouse. As the wounded man fell, his horse dragged him through town to the Preston Mansion. The horse stopped on the lawn while some of the ladies ran out to rescue him. They carried him upstairs to this room where he was pronounced 'dead.' The body was laid on the floor at the foot of the bed, where it remained for three days. An assistant and a nurse entered the room one afternoon. They noticed the body moving under its cover. The aide pulled the cover off the soldier's head.

"'Help me, help me,' he feebly begged them. As the two people gently rolled him over to be more comfortable, life seemed to drift back into him. The odor of rotting flesh was horrible! His wounds were bad, especially in his leg. Eventually, the Confederate said his name was Johnny and that he was from North Carolina. The doctor worked with Johnny a while, doing all he could to save him. Yet, late that night the young man died in that room."

We left Suite 300 behind. Our tour went up another flight of steps to the fourth floor. I asked Pete to tell me the legend of the horse which roams the lawn from time to time.

Pete vividly recalls the incident as it's recorded in Abingdon's history. "During the town's first invasion by Federal troops, many of the buildings were burned. As the invading soldiers left town, three Yankee sympathizers followed behind. Two of them escaped. But one was less fortunate. He rode past the courthouse toward the college; Confederate soldiers followed in dramatic pursuit. The Yankee rode into the alley east of the old gymnasium. As he did a gun battle erupted. Suddenly he was hit by a Confederate bullet. Only a short distance up the alley, he fell from his horse. The animal, also wounded, was badly frightened as well. It ran wildly on the campus grounds.

"The Yankee was brought into the parlor to the left of the front door. This was frequently used as an operating room during the war. Here the man survived a short while. In the meantime, his horse snorted and whinnied and paced on the front lawn. Some people tried to catch it; some wanted to shoot it to put it out of its pain. But no one could reach it. Late that night the horse awakened the nurses with its neighing."

According to the legend on nights when the moon is full and the sky is clear, that same riderless horse may be found roaming among the trees on campus. One exact sighting was by Pete's grandfather in 1935. Another report of the horse was in the 1970's. Seven employees of the bar were leaving at night when they entered the parking lot area behind the hotel. In front of them all patiently waited the riderless horse still looking for his owner.

"Alright, here's room 403," Pete announced as he selected the proper key. "This is Beth's room—where the soldier she fell in love with died." I entered the room which felt cozy and inviting. I was anxious to hear more about this place which seemingly was so active.

"February of this year, a security guard was in the main dining room, the First Lady's Table. He encountered the ghost of a woman in the hallway there. He thought she was a guest and asked, 'Can I help you, Ma'am?' Suddenly, he could see it was a spirit, not a solid, living person!" Pete described.

"The guard yelled into his two-way radio for help from the desk clerks on night duty. They thought he was joking. The spirit quickly ran up the steps by the gift shop and toward the East Parlors and swirled around in the lobby. One of the desk clerks met it face-to-face in the front hall. She screamed and hid behind the lobby desk.

"The image continued up the spiral staircase with the security guard after it. Briefly, the ghost stopped at the bend in the stairs to peer around it at the guard. As he was not far behind, both continued their chase further up the stairs. On the third floor landing is a huge gold-gilt mirror. In the reflection of this mirror, the guard watched the spirit pass through the solid door leading into room 403. Deciding that the room wouldn't be big enough for both of them, the guard ran outside with a pair of field glasses. From the yard below, he watched the ghostly image pace around the room. It wasn't until the following day that the guard found the courage to enter 403. The bedspread was wrinkled and some of the furniture had been shifted in what was an 'unoccupied' room."

Beth's room is possibly the most popular among guests and certainly the most famous. Where it may be somewhat smaller than some, it offers a quality of intimacy where one can readily picture a young, beautiful nurse falling in love with a pitiful, wounded soldier.

The bell captain resumed his narration on recent events in 403. "A police convention was held here late this spring. One state policeman from Arlington, Virginia stayed here accompanied by his wife. She was lying on the bed while he was getting ready to go to a meeting. The man had been in the bathroom taking a shower, creating a steamy atmosphere. As the policeman emerged from the shower, he was startled by the scene. Beth's name was scrawled on the mirror attached to the back of the bathroom door.

"The man yelled at his wife who he assumed was playing a joke on him. But, she'd had no part of it. She had slept soundly through it all," said Pete.

Pete is definitely "keeper of the tales" of the Martha Washington. Nearly everyone who experiences the "unusual" recounts it to Pete. There was much more to tell. "Two years ago during the time of the Highland Festival, another drama unfolded in room 403. One of our daytime housekeepers was cleaning this area. She went out in the hall to get towels. As she reentered 403, a heavy, filmy veil floated directly over the bed. The woman screamed for help.

"Other employees nearby came rushing in to see what the problem was. They saw the veil, too, before it disappeared. As evidence of its pressure, a large indentation remained on the bedspread long after the spirit's departure," he continued.

We walked across the hall to room 405. In this room we see the bed donated by Gloria Swanson in 1960. Miss Swanson frequently stayed at the Martha Washington Inn while visiting the famous Barter Theater in the 1930's. She was a strong supporter of the theater and donated many props for its performances.

Pete revealed more history of the Barter Theater. "It now owns the building that it's located in across the street. Also, the building without a roof over there beside the hotel was once the old Martha Washington College swimming pool, built in the early 19th century. Nearby that spot was the old Stonewall Jackson College, a Presbyterian ladies' college which burned down about 1910-1912. From there you can see the building on the end which is now the Barter Playhouse, but was originally part of the Stonewall Jackson College.

"I've heard that the theater is haunted, too," Pete declared. "Through the years several actors and actresses have come to me with strange stories. In fact, just this summer one of today's more popular actresses who played in the "Singing Nun" came to me with one. She was having dinner at the First Lady's Table when she told me about her experience just that afternoon before her matinée performance. As she entered her dressing room located directly under the stage, she felt 'something funny.' She was certain that someone was walking with her. Yet, when she turned to look around, no one was in sight. Only minutes after that, some stagehands came along in the hall outside her door. One of them yelled, then ran upstairs. He had distinctly seen the actress' ghost companion."

The Jeb Stuart Suite, number 400, is also located on the fourth floor. As one might guess, it honors Stuart with much memorabilia and photographs of that cavalier. It's in these rooms that more of the trap doors begin leading into the tunnels. These are near and behind the suite's closets. "These areas have had some pretty unusual things reported about them, too," said my guide. I wandered around investigating possible entrances to those legendary, mysterious tunnels. My curiosity raced wildly as to what might be found down in those secret passages today.

"But, let's walk back downstairs toward the Preston Suite." Pete resumed his words. "This past June a man and wife who had stayed there two nights came to me on the front porch. The couple had just returned from the Barter Theater. I noticed him studying me a bit; then he finally decided to confide in me, 'Mr. Sheffey, is this place haunted?'

"'Yes, sir, it is,' I'd answered." Then the guest proceeded to describe their experience from the previous night. "About 2:00 a.m. all the lights had come on spontaneously in the entire suite. They had thought someone had mistakenly entered their room. The man got out of bed, looked around, even called a security guard. But, no one had invaded their privacy. Soon they turned off the lights, except the bathroom one, and retired again.

"Later that same night, his wife awakened again to find that every one of the lights was on again. The husband insisted that he could feel cold spots and areas of heavy pressure at the time." Pete assured the guest that he, too, was familiar with those sensations, but that all was safe and well at the inn.

Our walk through the elegant rooms and parlors was coming to a close. We descended the Colonial staircase which had seen so much passage of history, and again we stood in the front hallway. "Since we're at this point, I'll tell you of another incident three years ago. The night auditor was on duty at the desk here. She heard something running up and down the hall near the ballroom and through the East Parlors. Thinking that it was someone's pet and aware that none are allowed here, she went to capture the source of the ruckus.

"She made it to the marble table here beside us, when suddenly she encountered a swirling ball of cloudy energy on the bottom step of the stairway! The auditor froze to the spot. Her assistant still behind the desk, could remember trying to wake up and not being able to. Very soon the morning cook entered the front door. Suddenly the spirit shot up the spiral staircase!"

We walked by Small Pleasures, and Janice Oliver, the owner, was at its doorway. I couldn't resist asking her about any ghostly apparitions around the gift shop. Janice replied charmingly, "I took over the shop on May 1, 1994. I haven't seen any ghosts yet." She thought a bit on events those first days. "But several days, early in the morning as I entered the shop, I would find all of the Civil War and ghost books on the floor instead of shelves where they were kept in the smaller room to one side. Often, they would fly off the shelf with no one around to cause it." Now that Janice has moved them out to the larger room in a more prominent display, this activity has ceased.

Even more recently Pete became aware of an occurrence regarding music. He explained what happened. "Two weeks ago on a Thursday night, another auditor heard music playing mysteriously in the upper hallways above the staircase. At 5:00 a.m. he'd been awakened by music in the East Parlor. He approached the closed door and stood listening. As he opened the door and turned on the lights, the sounds ceased abruptly. Not only was the room unoccupied, but there was no musical instrument to produce the sounds."

Were these the same melancholy violin strains which Beth played for Captain John Toves? The visitors must decide for themselves. By all means, visit the Martha for a magnificent trip back through bygone legends. As time came for me to leave, a sadness came over me, as though an old friend was being left behind.

John Barleycorn Himself

Edwin K. Stout, 85, of 203 Webster Street, Clarksburg, W.Va. was an eyewitness to the death of the first man killed in the Civil War. July 7, 1929 the "Sunday Exponent Telegram" reported his accurate version of the experience. Mr. Stout was the only man still living who witnessed it, and recounts it quite differently from the way history records it:

T. Bailey Brown, a member of Capt. Daniel Wilson's company of the Union forces, was the man killed. W.S. Knight, a member of one of the two companies which had come from Highland County, Va. to Grafton to assist Col. George Porterfield in recruiting soldiers for the Southern army and in efforts to sway the tide against secession in northwestern Virginia was the man who did the killing.

The killing took place the evening of May 22, 1861, at Fetterman, now part of Grafton.

Mr. Stout innocently spoke the single word, which resulted in the rifling, when as a picket he cried: 'Halt!" to Brown.

The narrative by Mr. Stout of the affair as he recalls it at this late date holds one's attention.

On Picket Duty

Mr. Stout, who was only 17 years old at the time, had voluntarily dropped in with Capt. Warren S. Lurty's company of men as they passed through Bridgeport, Stout's home town, to join the Porterfield forces at Grafton. Along with the late James McCann, of Bridgeport, and Benjamin Corder, both slightly older than Stout, he was assigned to picket duty at the east end of the Fetterman bridge across the Tygarts Valley River.

"Billy" Knight was standing sentinel on the east side of the railroad crossing a short distance from the bridge, as shown by a marker since erected there.

"We did not know what we were there for," Mr. Stout says. "But there were crowded traffic conditions on the bridge, and I suppose we were placed there as traffic pickets. At any rate it was our duty to keep the bridge clear. Knight was a lookout for evidence of any advance of Union forces which were expected at any time from the state of Ohio.

"Brown, the man who was killed, had come down from Grafton, to where Knight was and they engaged in a conversation, as they knew one another. Brown had been drinking and was 'fool' full. Knight told him not to 'go down that way,' but to go on home above Grafton toward Flemington, where they both lived.

"When the drunken man crossed the railroad track, Knight remarked to him, 'you should better not go over as you will get into trouble' and again entreated him to go home, telling him if he did not, 'some one will hurt you.'

Advice Unheeded

"Making an offhand remark to the effect, 'Oh, hell, I can whip the whole damn crowd,' Brown declined to heed the advice, and then Knight said 'you better take my word and go back the other way or you will surely get hurt.'

"The drunken man then came toward the bridge and I called 'Halt!' as I was standing there as a picket. He immediately whirled around, raised his gun and shot at Knight, evidently believing that he was the one who had commanded him to halt. The bullet struck Knight on one side of his cheeks, clipped off a piece of his ear and glanced along the side of the head in the rear of the ear."

Knight returned the fire with a smooth-bore musket loaded with slugs, killing Brown instantly.

"The ball," Mr. Stout says, "entered the lower left side and come out at the right shoulder. Brown threw up his hands and fell. A crowd gathered around the fallen man and he was carried off into a room in the upstairs of a school building not far away, where a consultation was held but no action taken. Knight gave himself up, but there were no proceedings against him so far as I learned.

ℳade ℋo Statement

"I had never seen either man before that day and never saw Knight afterwards. I never was asked to make any statement to any of the officials about the shooting as it was treated as a mere incident of war.

"Soon after that I returned home but McCann and Bender later went south and fought in the Confederate army. At the same time my uncle, Mortimer Johnson, who lived at Pruntytown and was a brother of the late John C. Johnson, went with the Confederate forces. His wife and Mrs. Kemble, a relative, were later taken by my father, James Pindall Stout, in a spring wagon from Beverly to Staunton, where they remained during the remainder of the war. He had been given a pass through the lines by the Union commander, Gen. George McCellan in 1862,"

Some time after the battle at Philippi, June 3, 1861, in which the Confederates were routed, Mr. Stout, in company which Chapin Barlett and Richard Johnson, youngest brother of the late John K. Johnson, decided to make their way through the mountains into Virginia to join the Southern forces.

Mounted, they went across the country by way of Pruntytown to the ferry crossing on the Tygarts Valley River at Nicklow between Grafton and Philippi. They had no trouble in crossing the river as they were not suspected by the ferryman. They proceeded until they reached the top of the mountains, fully bent on their mission, little suspecting that they would shortly have a change of front.

Union Encampment

As they reached the top of the mountains, they glanced down over its banks and were startled to see an encampment of Union soldiers. Panic-stricken, they whirled their horses, lashed them to the limit and came down the mountain side at full speed, but they had been seen by the enemy and their sudden turning caused a detachment of men to rush up from the Union camp to the top of the mountains where they fired repeatedly at the three unnerved "musketeers."

Mr. Stout was riding a fine Morgan racing stallion, Johnson was mounted on a fine racing mare and Bartlett had a "pretty good" plug. Coming to a long slope of mountain road, "we made our horses do their best," Mr. Stout said. "Union soldiers were at the top of the mountain firing at us and we imagined we could hear the bullets whirring over our heads. Our racers never made better time."

Refused Assistance

Mr. Stout recalls that when "we came to the ferry, the old man in charge of the boat refused to ferry us across, as he said it meant sacrificing his life to do so. He told us there was the boat and we could do as we pleased about using it.

"As we preferred rather to face and fight the raging waters of the Tygarts Valley River, (it was on a rampage as the result of a freshet), than await the enemy, we accepted the old ferryman's suggestion to help ourselves to the ferry boat. I knew nothing about such a boat except that it should be headed in a certain way to reach the opposite bank.

"We rode onto the boat and pushed off for the other shore. We succeeded in approaching the opposite bank and grabbing the overhanging limbs of trees we finally landed from a quarter to a half mile down stream. After landing we separated and went to our respective homes. I arrived back home on the third day after I had left to join the army.

"That was the extent of my efforts to go to war, as after I reached home I stayed there and was a good boy after that."

Feared Raid

However, Mr. Stout had other experiences in the war. He not only fled toward home when the Union soldiers pursued him as just related, but he also headed for home in advance of a Confederate body of soldiers, fearing to face them too. Just before the Jones raid in 1863, Mr. Stout was attending school at the Morgantown Academy. A few days before the raiding army appeared in Morgantown, he was tipped off by a fellow student that Jones would be there within a week.

Mr. Stout realized that Gen. Jones and his men would not know who he was or that he was a Southern sympathizer and fearing harsh treatment, perhaps capture and imprisonment, he decided discretion the better part of valor and left for home just in time to precede the army raiders up from Fairmont.

The raiders left the main road at the mouth of Simpson Creek at Meadowbrook and passed up the Simpson Creek Road by the Stout home, which was about two miles below Bridgeport, and where Nathan Richards now lives. They foraged for horses and took many a farm animals away with them.

Horses Concealed

"Shortly before they passed our place, Father and I hitched our horses under the spreading limbs of a large hawthorn tree on the farm, beneath which the cattle had lain down in the heat of the day, and they were completely concealed from view. We walked back up hill and looking in the distance we saw the Confederate flag up the road about two miles away. Jones' troops were on their way back to Staunton. They were taking all the horses they could lay hands on, but they missed my same stallion which I had ridden on the attempt to join the Southern army as well as my father's horse, both safely hidden under the old hawthorn tree.

"When father saw the Rebels coming he remarked that he believed he would go up to Bridgeport and did so, walking along the railroad. I went home. They did not bother us."

Mr. Stout says he was arrested several times during the war, charged with being a spy, although he never engaged in any such work, he declares.

"I was frequently charged with 'giving aid and comfort' to the Confederates," Mr. Stout recalls. "I was never connected with the Southern armies and never served in their intelligence or information bureaus. I did, however, from time to time, share my bed with straggling Southern soldiers and give them something to eat when they applied.

Father Arrested

"At one time, Union soldiers arrested my father, myself and old Uncle Milton Weir who lived on our place, and brought us to Clarksburg, where we were taken before a Union colonel and asked what we were there for. I replied, 'I am here because I have no excuse for not being here. Union soldiers commanded me to come and I came.'

"I then asked why I was brought there, and was informed that I was accused of being a Rebel spy. Denying the charge, I informed the court or colonel that I had no connection with southern forces whatever. My word was accepted and I was released.

"When father, myself and Weir were arrested and brought in we were held prisoners at the old Walker house about a week, where we received royal treatment and had a good time," Mr. Stout says, in discussing the prison feature of his detention. "I was brought to the county jail once, but for some reason I was not put in, but taken into the court room instead for 'trial.'"

Others in the House.

In addition to his own party, Mr. Stout remembers there were several more corralled at the Walker house. Explaining the fine time they had, he said that Mrs. James M. Jackson, whose husband was among those being held, sent over cakes and wines and they all fared well. In all there were twenty-seven Harrison county Southern sympathizers there at the time, among whom besides Mr. Jackson was the late James M. Stout, father of Ross F. Stout, a former sheriff of the county.

A few of the suspects were later placed in jail but most of them were released under surveillance and permitted to return to their homes.

Richard Johnson, who rode away from home with Mr. Stout on military venture bent and who returned faster than he went as already told, and Benjamin Corder, who was a picket with Mr. Stout at the Fetterman Bridge when Bailey Brown was killed, both went south and were killed in battle for the "lost cause."

Mr. Stout says he has ever regretted the incident which resulted in the death of Brown, but he himself did only what every other man in his line of duty would have done and adds that "John Barleycorn" was really to blame.

The Wilson House

The gaping hole in the broken second-story window yawned menacingly at the two women. One long branch of an old oak tree had managed to find its way through the opening. For years, the oak had made the Wilson place its home, particularly this upstairs bedroom. Nearby, a jagged crack in the wall wound snake-like between the two windows. Ancient English ivy tendrils sneaked through from the outside, keeping company with the oak.

Margaret and her friend Betsy exchanged incredulous looks. "What did your landlord say about this room?" Betsy demanded to know.

Margaret slowly surveyed the deplorable looking room. She gradually found her voice. "Well, he said this room was in rough condition and needed some cleaning up before it could be used...but I never suspected this!"

"Yeh, it needs work all right," Betsy agreed sarcastically.

Margaret had already started to back out of the room. "Come on. Let's get out of here. We can start cleaning in another area. All we really need are two bedrooms to begin with. The kids are young enough that they're still happy sharing a bedroom."

Betsy followed behind her down the long hallway toward the steps. As they passed the largest room, she stopped to examine the heavy padlock on one door. "What's this for?" she asked.

"Mr. Wilson says there're old family things stored there that he doesn't have any place else to store. He asked me not to bother the locks. There's one on that door too." Margaret pointed toward the matching door at the end of the hall. "That's all one long room. Strange, huh?"

Betsy agreed. But something didn't set well with her. Something nagged in the back of her mind; yet she couldn't quite figure it out. She kept silent.

"Let's try this one," the other woman pushed open another door. This bedroom was more presentable. "Should we start in here?"

"Sure. The faster we get started, the more light we'll have. I don't think you have electricity. We won't be cleaning after dark." Betsy flipped a couple of light switches as she spoke. None of them worked.

Margaret replied, "You're right." She made a mental note to call the electric company the next morning. Both women set to the task of preparing the huge house for occupation. With broom in hand, Margaret recalled events leading her to this situation.

Her husband, an abusive drunkard, had finally gone too far. Margaret had finally moved out of their home near Marietta, Ohio after seven years of pure hell. Thanks to her wonderful friend Betsy, Margaret and the two boys had a place to seek refuge until they found a home they could afford. Margaret was determined to locate an apartment far enough away from her husband that he wouldn't find her.

Just when the situation seemed desperate, she drove past this empty old house. The "For Rent" sign had been in the yard in the weather for a while. Its lawn badly needed weeding and mowing. The size of it would have indicated a very high rent. But something about its appearance was compelling. Margaret copied the phone number from the sign and drove to the nearest phone.

Mr. Wilson answered her call. When asked about the rent, he paused noticeably. "Well,...that's somewhat negotiable. Let me come out there and show you around the place."

Margaret agreed to meet him back at the vacant house within half an hour. During her wait, she sized up the yard. Yes, lots of space for the boys to play, and there was practically no traffic on the street. She could put them to work helping to clear the small branches and debris from the yard. The house looked as though it had sat empty for quite a while. Still, the owner said the rent was "negotiable," and that appealed to Margaret.

A tall, thin, elderly man got out of the car which he parked in front of the house. "Hi there. I'm Wilson." He stretched out his lean arm to shake her hand. The sight of his yellowed talon-like finger-nails made Margaret's skin crawl.

She gingerly shook his hand and introduced herself. "My two

young sons and I need a place to rent for a while." She briefly explained the situation to him, emphasizing how she couldn't afford much rent.

"Well, come on inside and have a look. She isn't much to see now, but at one time she was a beauty. You see, we don't get many renters these days, so it's been empty a few years. The house has been in my family for quite a while, and I own the one I live in downtown." He unlocked the front door, and both of them entered the once elegant hallway.

Margaret was impressed with what she saw. Indeed, the house had been grand. Dust cloths covered everything in sight, which was a fairly extensive display of furniture. Mr. Wilson escorted her from room to room, giving her ample time to survey the house.

Next, they went upstairs where he casually opened the door of the room at the top of the steps. "This is pretty much what all these rooms up here are like. That one at the end of the hall requires extra attention; also the largest one is to always remain locked. Mr. Wilson quickly ended the upstairs tour. "That's about it for the second floor." He led the way back down the steps.

Once back in the hallway, Margaret raised the question of money. "What amount would you consider fair for rent?" she asked him directly.

The man ran his hands through his thinning hair. Again Margaret flinched. "How does $300 a month sound to you?" he responded.

The woman couldn't believe her ears. True, the house needed extensive cleaning before she could move in. But that was cheap rent for such a place fully furnished. She knew she could depend on Betsy to help her with moving details. "I'll take it."

The deal was sealed. The landlord handed over the keys while Margaret wrote a check for rent. Now, two days later, she and her best friend tried to make the place livable.

Mark and Daniel went through their usual foolishness before going to bed. Each had his individual way of avoiding going to sleep. Finally, Margaret was able to tuck them in. She sat close by the two beds until their sleepy eyes slid shut.

Softly, Margaret tiptoed out of the room and headed toward the staircase. Instead of turning the overhead light on, she left on a small lamp in the long hallway. It was dimly lit, but enough illumination to see by when she returned upstairs. As she walked past the padlocked room, that same sensation of curiosity moved through her thoughts.

She reached for the railing at the top of the steps and paused momentarily. Something behind her caught her attention. As Margaret stepped down to the top step she saw a black blur of motion at the far end of the hall. Her heart skipped a beat. Margaret hoped she was imagining things.

Suddenly, she realized she wasn't. Coming directly toward her was the full figure of a woman dressed in a floor-length black crinoline gown. The appearance was that of a female in mourning clothes. It floated about a foot above the floor, and moved silently toward Margaret.

She heard someone scream, and realized the sound came from her own throat. Margaret felt frozen to the spot. As the apparition got closer, Margaret could see the dark hair parted in the center and made up in a bun. A faint, thin veil covered its face. She was watching a phantom from the 1800s, suspended in grief.

Just before the spirit reached the stairway, it dissipated into vapor as smoke would waft away. At this point both boys came out of their room. They recognized fear on their mother's face. The pair ran toward her and ran directly through the fading wisps of the lady in mourning. "What's wrong, Momma? Why is it so cold out here in the hall?"

Margaret hadn't noticed the deadly cold at all until now. "Well, I don't know about the cold, Son. But, I think it's time for us to get out of this place."

The boys looked confused, yet they obeyed their mother. They returned to their bedroom and got clothes and items for tomorrow. "Are we going to stay at Betsy's tonight?" Daniel wondered.

"Yes, that's exactly what we'll do," Margaret responded. She ushered her boys downstairs and outside toward the car. Tonight they would barge in on Betsy. Margaret knew she would understand. In the back of her mind, however, she was determined to return to the upstairs of the old house. Agreement or not, tomorrow she would see for herself what lay behind those padlocked doors.

The two women stared at the lock. "This might not be so difficult after all," declared Betsy. "Look at how old these bolts are." She fingered the plate which held the latch on. Even though the lock itself was recent, all the metal around it was old and rusty.

"We'll soon find out," came Margaret's retort. With this, she started pounding away at the latch with the hammer they had brought.

It only took four stout whacks to cause the entire mechanism to fall away. The intruders exchanged looks. Now nothing stood in their way. Flashes of last night's visitor floated across Margaret memory. Still, she seemed determined.

The wooden door swung open, and Margaret stepped through. The early morning light partially illuminated the room. Shelves with bottles and jars and utensils lined the wall across from her. She read the labels aloud, "Zinc chloride, alcohol, mercuric chloride, formaldehyde...Look at all those pans and trays, Betsy. This looks like some kind of laboratory."

Then Betsy grabbed Margaret on the arm. As she turned to her friend, Betsy pointed toward a dark corner at the end of the room. A large sign leaned against the wall. "Wilson's Funeral Home" it read. That was all they needed to see.

Many months later, long after Margaret and her sons had moved out, she mustered up the courage to return at least to the outside of the Wilson house. She was drawn to the overgrown backyard. Once there, a small grove of trees compelled her to explore further.

Finally, Margaret spotted what she was searching for. Midst the gnarled confusion of undergrowth were tombstones from years ago. Names and dates were inconsistent. Yet, she was able to read such dates as 1859, 1863, and 1866.

The house was mysterious to everyone in town. No one confessed to really knowing the history of the place. But one thing was certain among the townsfolk. The stately mansion had stood there before the Civil War began.

Fort Pulaski

Fort Pulaski serves not only as a memorial to the valor and dedication of those connected with its construction, bombardment, and defense, but also as a history lesson on the elusiveness of invincibility.

Construction of the fort began in 1831 after Second Lieutenant Robert E. Lee, having just graduated as a young engineering officer from West Point, surveyed the fort site in 1829. Lee also designed the dike system necessary for draining and protecting the construction area. Located on Cockspur Island about eighteen miles from Savannah, Georgia, Fort Pulaski is similar in size to Fort Sumter. It encloses five acres of land. The brick walls are seven and a half feet thick and thirty-five feet high, surrounded by a moat seven feet deep and thirty-five feet wide.

At the outbreak of the Civil War, Fort Pulaski was manned only by an ordnance sergeant and a caretaker. However, on January 3, 1861 Georgians landed on Cockspur Island and raised the state flag. Repairs and upgrading began.

Not far away on November 7, 1861, Union forces captured Hilton Head Island. General Sherman then began his seize-and-capture plans for Fort Pulaski. Confederate troops retreated southward from Tybee Island as Union troops led by Captain Gillmore moved in. Gillmore was a staunch proponent of the accuracy, as well as the power, of rifled cannon. Unlike smoothbore cannon, rifled guns have spiraled grooves inside the barrel. These grooves cause the projectile to spin as it emerges, thus increasing its accuracy, as well as its range and penetration power.

To this time rifled cannon had not been used successfully beyond six hundred yards. The Union forces now on Tybee Island were more than a mile from the fort. Military history supported Robert E. Lee's remark to Colonel Olmstead, commander of the fort, speaking with reference to the Union guns that would, "make it pretty warm for you here with shells, but they cannot breach your walls at that distance."

At 8:10 a.m. on April 10, 1862 Colonel Olmstead commanded 385 men of five Georgia infantries. At this time the first Union 197 pound shell was lofted over Pulaski, followed by further rifle, cannon and Columbiads. All of these picked away at the brickwork of the masonry walls. Much to the surprise of everyone involved, the Confederates surrendered at 2:30 p.m. on the 11th of April. Federal bombardments had enlarged a smaller breech at the southeast angle of the fort. What lay straight ahead of the missiles was a powder magazine housing four-thousand pounds of powder. Further fighting would be disastrous.

Through the remainder of the war, Union troops occupied Fort Pulaski to support the blockade. Because of their somewhat precarious position midst the deep South, Federal troops used the fort as a prison for the Immortal Six-Hundred, as well as others. These six-hundred were senior enlisted men, mainly Confederate officers, used as human shields to prevent Confederate troops from firing on Fort Pulaski during Federal occupation. The Immortal Six-Hundred were originally imprisoned at Fort Delaware, Point Lookout, and Elmira, N.Y. but were relocated to Fort Pulaski specifically for this purpose.

Many reenactors have celebrated anniversary events at the fort. But for the 125th Anniversary, several Georgia units gathered to honor Fort Pulaski and her men in a special way. Reenactors came from Atlanta, the 1st Georgia Infantry was there, as well as members of the Georgia Division of the Reenactors Association. The participants elected to create an unusual event without the presence of the general public. This would be an "Answer For Them Formation."

Thomas, one of the commanders present, explains how this is done. "We had volunteers do a lot of research on particular battles. One large battle from East or West was chosen, then a smaller battle or skirmish from the other area was chosen as well. So instead of calling roll, we called a date, such as 1862-Battle of Second Manassas. At this time another man would stand and remind them of the smaller fight too, including the number of casualties. This way we remember the guys who fought in some of the lesser-known places."

The "Answer For Them Formation" had begun and it was taking a little time to complete. Thomas describes the scene that followed, "Suddenly, this huge, thick cloud moved in through the entire fort. Honest to God, it really looked like a bad, bad Hollywood movie. It moved in so quickly and thick through the inside of the fort, rolling up though the windows like dry ice. This was big-time fog! By the time we got to calling out the year 1865, it was so thick that we couldn't see more than five feet in front of us. We were strictly going by voices. Then from the battles mentioned at 1865, we talked about the end of the war and the surrender of forces after Appomattox. Two seconds later that entire fog was completely gone! The sun was out, and it looked as though the fog had never been there." Thomas has lived along the coast many years and is familiar with erratic weather patterns. He exclaims, "But this was so incredibly dramatic and the timing of it was too perfect! Normally, after an event portrayal, we will go inside, reminisce, tell stories. Not that night though—everyone was affected by the 'fog.'"

1988 was the 126th Anniversary of the surrender of Fort Pulaski. Again, most of the same Georgia reenactors were present to stage an event, this time to include the public. Candlelight tours were arranged so that people could observe from room-to-room the progression of events of many years previous. First, the visitor was shown the guardroom, then all of the various quarters, the kitchen, the surgeon's quarters and finally a casemate. In each area the reenactors displayed a specific scenario that ran from the very taking of the fort by Georgia forces to after the siege.

One portrayal was of the Irish Jasper Greens (1st Georgia Infantry) and how they turned in their original uniforms. Blue fabric piped in green were convict colors in Ireland. Refusing to wear the uniforms of convicts, their colors were changed to gray with green.

The next scenario was two officers speaking to another gentleman. One officer had had more "traditional" war experience. He was declaring how this would be a "long, bloody war."

Beyond that was an especially effective scene. The reenactor portraying a surgeon had just gotten engaged to the woman posing as the wife of an ill soldier. Everyone involved was sitting in the same room; consequently a directional candle shone on the person speaking in order to change the audience's attention. This also served to make the room seem like two different places. There was an exchange of letters between the soldier's wife and the surgeon, regarding her husband's health. Unfortunately, their last two letters crossed in the mail. The woman's letter to the surgeon, asking him to remind her husband to be brave and get well, passed the surgeon's letter announcing his death. Because of the strong emotional tie between the two in real life, there wasn't a dry eye in the room.

In the last room was a portrayal of the Confederate men under guard as prisoners after Fort Pulaski was surrendered. One group was giving the colonel a difficult time for giving up so easily. The colonel is left to explain why he had to do so. Because of the Irish and other European descent of these soldiers, they didn't have fond memories of being rebels. In Ireland rebels were nearly always shot or hung after their capture. Yet, the American-born men were attempting to convince them that they would be treated well.

The visitors were next escorted to the parade ground. Thomas, reenacting with the 1st Georgia Infantry, was again present. He describes the activities as they continued. "Pulaski is very unique in that we know exactly by name who was walking the guard posts at what hour, at which location, and carrying exact equipment, during that entire time-span previous to and during the Civil War. This particular evening we put our men up on duty so that the visitors can observe. We asked them to, 'please stay silent and listen a short while.'

"After several tours through the evening, we'd gotten to the last one about 10:30 p.m. All of the visitors, as well as our people from the inside rooms, had collected outside to conclude the evening. We could see the guards walking with their candle lanterns. We had only five men to post on the six guard posts. So the sixth one had been vacant all evening. The Corporal of the Guard emerged from the guardhouse to say, 'Guard posts report and report here.'

"Each of the guards walked back carrying his lighted candle lantern, beginning with post number one, followed by the other four. I wanted to thank everyone for attending. But before I could say anything, someone in the crowd of about fifty people asked, 'What's that?' She was pointing upward to guard post number six.

"At the unattended post was a light moving as though carried by a man. As clear as a bell, everyone heard, 'Guard post number six, all's well!' With that, the light went out. We did a quick head count of park personnel, and everyone else who should have been present. No one could account for the extra guard on duty," Thomas assures me.

Every two years, the ladies of the Georgia reenactment units have frightening difficulty with one special closet door. When the women attend these events at Fort Pulaski, they stay overnight in the bachelor officers' quarters. The closet in those quarters gets used as a changing room. Very frequently someone gets locked in, and no one on the outside can help her out.

In anticipation of this, the reenactors request the key from the park service ahead of time. The key is tested; it always works fine...until one of the women enters the closet. Talley has to be called in from Savannah. He drives eighteen miles out to the fort, pounds and pull on the door, then it opens.

Some of these strange occurrences and feelings also strike people in the dark confines of the prison there. At one point in Pulaski's history, two soldier prisoners had escaped. Upon their capture the pair was returned and thrown into these dark confines.

The black stairwell of the fort seems to harbor similar sensations. Long ago a soldier fell down those stairs, hitting his head. There he died from those head traumas.

Sarah Winchester

"That damned Yankee rifle that can be loaded on Sunday and be fired all week," could be heard by many a Confederate soldier during the Civil War. Such was one description of the Henry Repeater, the first magazine rifle used in high quantity by the Union army. 1,731 Henry Repeaters and 4,610,400 Henry cartridges were purchased by the government during the war from July 23, 1863 to November 7, 1865.

Thousands of Confederate soldiers were killed or maimed by this weapon during the war. In one instance, two regiments of Sherman's army in their march to the sea under Major General Dodge's command, were fully armed with the Henry rifles.

Invented by B. Tyler Henry and patented October 16, 1860, it was manufactured by the New Haven Arms Company of Connecticut. While this company did not bear the Winchester name, Oliver F. Winchester, a New Haven shirt manufacturer, was the principal stockholder.

The original design of the Henry was improved upon in 1866. The capability to load the magazine through the gate in the right-hand side of the frame became possible. This newer gun became the Winchester Model 1866. During the same year the Winchester Repeating Arms Co. was formed out of the reorganization of the New Haven Arms Co.

Carey easily entered the front door. For years after her family moved away, the former home of Sarah Winchester welcomed Carey

Hovey and always opened its doors on her occasional visits. Carey's brothers had remained in the San Francisco Bay area for years after their family sold the Winchester home to a group of investors who intended to "fix it up," "renovate it," and essentially turn it into a Yuppie version of Victorian-style. By modernizing it, they felt assured of tripling their money at the height of the California real estate boom.

Carey looked around in sadness. The original white paint of the exterior was painted over in a three-tone muddy pink color scheme. Here and there blue trim made it look like a prop in a horror movie. Carey's mother, Anna, had been quite loyal to the integrity of the Classic Victorian home. The previously boarded-over kitchen fireplace was reopened and restored. Anna had removed the old wallpaper covering the gorgeous hand-planed redwood walls of the library. But the newer contractors had arrived and immediately gutted the restored kitchen. The idea was to make it "functional" they claimed. One of the original bedrooms was remodeled, creating a master bathroom with jacuzzi. Next, the Victorian gardens were torn out. Carey had lovingly tended the old rosemary bushes and lilacs of the original period. Instead, the investors had mulched the yard and planted trimmed junipers accompanied by highlight lamps.

Neighbors and friends kept Carey's family informed of the status of the Winchester house. It sat empty and unsold for years. The investors would come to check on it and would find previously locked doors standing wide open. Many windows originally secured, would be unlocked and wide open. The Spirits frequently showed their distaste for the new owners. Gradually, the investors "lost their shirts" with the deal.

It sat alone at the end of a road lined on either side with large oak trees. The aged Los Altos house had had a reputation for years among the townspeople as being haunted. At one short time it had been a school. Afterward, another family maintained it as their residence before the Hovey family's purchase. But again, the house would remain vacant for years before Carey's family found it.

When the summer of 1969 arrived, the Hoveys moved into Sarah Winchester's former home. They soon learned of Sarah's history. She had purchased it in the early 1880's. To the original two-room wooden frame house, Sarah had added large Victorian sections, a beautiful front stairway, hallways, a living room with high ceilings, more bedrooms, and a formal dining room.

Sarah and her sister Elizabeth Merriman lived here while construction began on yet another house—now quite famous. Sarah Winchester, a very spiritual and strong-willed woman, had always felt remorse about the Civil War. It was her husband Oliver F. Winchester who had financed the creation of so many weapons of destruction, both the Henry Repeater, as well as the Winchester Rifle.

Following her husband's death, Sarah had a spiritual reading done. The "reader" said that she was to take the fortune inherited from these weapons of death and build a structure "to house the Spirits of everyone ever killed by her husband's guns." Sarah took this information to heart. She soon began design and construction on the famous Winchester Mystery House in San Jose, California. It contains countless rooms of unusual angles, stairways leading nowhere, and doors which open to empty space. Visitors travel hundreds of miles to see this tribute to the Winchester fortune.

However, it seems that the energy and spirit of Sarah Winchester clings to the home in Los Altos. This first became evident to Mrs. Hovey one afternoon while she was "alone." She was in an upstairs room when the distinct odor of old English roses or rose perfume surrounded her. Immediately, Anna assumed that it had wafted in from outdoors. Yet, as she looked around, she saw that all of the windows and doors were closed. The sweet smell lingered a bit and gradually dissipated. After the family returned that afternoon, Mrs. Hovey reserved her thoughts on the occurrence, deciding not to share them right away.

It wasn't long into the week before each of the Hoveys had his or her separate experiences with a visitation involving the pleasant odor of roses. Never did they feel threatened. But every night for an extended period of time, when the youngsters were in bed, around 11:30 Mr. and Mrs. Hovey would clearly hear footsteps walking up and down the hallway downstairs. There was never anyone in sight.

One afternoon in particular, Anna was again "alone" upstairs and was expecting her neighbor to come visit. "Anna...Anna..." came the lilting voice calling her name from downstairs.

"I'm up here; I'm coming down," Anna replied.

"Anna...Anna...," again called the gentle voice.

Mrs. Hovey hurried down the stairs to greet her guest. Once on the landing she realized that no one was there.. She stood alone, searching for the invisible visitor.

Christmas for the Hoveys was always a festive occasion with old-fashioned decorations and frequent visitors. The family was gathered near the tree one evening when suddenly the antique sleigh bells hanging outside the front door began jingling loudly. Of course, when Carey went out to greet their visitor, no one could be seen. Not even a breeze was evident to cause the stir.

That same Christmas week while the family was gathered, each person chose a separate room for wrapping gifts. Suddenly, everyone heard a very obnoxious banging in part of the house. Each person experienced it as being in a different location. Carey who was upstairs was certain that it came from downstairs. Everyone downstairs was sure it was Carey on the upper level. The loud noise continued until the family rushed to the stair landing, gathering to locate and stop the commotion. Finally, it became obvious that it came from within the walls of the house. The disturbance ceased as abruptly as it began and never returned.

The situation during the following Christmas was somewhat more dramatic. More relatives came to visit—aunts, grandmothers, cousins, all converged at once. All were gathered this evening in the library for noisy, animated conversation. In this room, which was part of the older section, there was a small fireplace of Italian marble. Sarah had proudly ordered the marble shipped around Cape Horn to be installed in her library. On the mantel over the fireplace, the Hoveys displayed two antique, toy brass cannons.

Carey and her mother stood in a room nearby when they heard horrible screaming and footsteps running from the library. They rushed toward their guests' room to see what was happening. One of the heavy cannons had levitated several inches in mid-air over the mantelpiece and flung itself across the room toward the loudest voice.

Nevertheless, the Hoveys remained content with Sarah Winchester's house. Enough so, that Anna reached an agreement with the spirits sharing the space. At the point when their activities seemed to increase, Anna stood in the main hallway and announced in a very loud, clear voice, "We're intending to live in this house, but we can't if there are going to be problems with it. I'll make a deal with whoever else lives here. We'll leave you alone, and you leave us alone. Everyone will live in peace. If we are forced to sell the house, then considering the financial situation here in Silicon Valley, I can guarantee that it will be torn down and a subdivision will be built in its place. You spirits will have no place to go because old houses are becoming scarce. Nobody wants that to happen."

For the most part, the activities ceased except for the occasional smell of old roses—just a hint to remind the Hoveys that the spirits were alive and well. Anna kept her end of the bargain, as well. Through the years psychics and curiosity-seekers approached her for permission to do séances there and to tour the house. But Mrs. Hovey stood firm. Not only did she refuse the offers, she wouldn't even discuss the idea.

The Winchester house had always been dominated by women, primarily those of strong convictions. Sarah and her sister had frequently opened their doors to unwed mothers, allowing them to stay and give birth in their home. During the building of the railroad, the two sisters would sneak out at night and pull up the surveyors' markers. They were terribly opposed to the railroad running through town. The next day the surveyors would have to do it again. Two nights later Sarah and Isabelle would again remove the markers. The women were quite particular about what happened in their town, as well as their home. To this day they remain particular about who lives in their house and how it is maintained.

"In great deeds something abides. On great fields something stays. Forms change and pass, bodies disappeared; but spirits linger, to consecrate ground for the vision-place of souls. And reverent men and women from afar, and generations that know us not and that we know not of, heart-drawn to see where and by whom great things were suffered and done for them, shall come to this deathless field, to ponder and dream; and lo! the shadow of a mighty presence shall wrap them in its bosom, and the power of the vision pass into their souls."

General Joshua Lawrence Chamberlain, Gettysburg,
    October 3, 1889

Virgil's Story

Five of us gathered at Gettysburg the weekend of February 11, 1995. Uncertain of what would happen, each was excited to be there, especially at a time when few tourists visited. We would essentially have the Gettysburg Battlefield to ourselves. Or, would we?

Michael Flood, a Confederate reenactor and a corrections officer with the state of New York, arrived Friday evening with his girl-friend, Barbara Doeinck, a registered nurse also with the New York Correctional System. They checked into one of the inns located on the edge of the battlefield park and then went on to dinner. Because of their long drive, the two retired early.

3:12 a.m. read the clock by the bed. Michael looked around, abruptly awakened from his sound sleep. Someone had firmly tapped three times on his left shoulder. He looked toward Barbara who was fast asleep. Nowhere in the room were there signs of who had awakened him. Somewhat perplexed, Michael went back to sleep.

4:23 a.m. Barbara and Michael were rudely awakened by the sounds of her car alarm going off. Michael leaped from bed, grabbed the car keys, and silenced the alarm. Again, there was no one in sight to have caused the disturbance. Suddenly, Michael heard two "booms" followed by more firing of what seemed like cannons. He felt as though he was witnessing an artillery attack on Gettysburg! The barrage of cannon fire continued another ten minutes!

4:33 a.m. five or six soldiers presented themselves in Michael's room. To use his own words, "It sounds unbelievable, but I was awake, and I know it happened. Although I couldn't exactly see anyone, I knew they were there. They communicated with me through a sort of thought transference.

"One soldier who was most likely in charge," Michael further explains, "started speaking to me, 'What are you doing here? Why are you wearing grey? Where is your musket?'

"After answering these questions, I asked some of my own," says Michael. "'Why did you set the car alarm off?'"

The Civil War soldier responded matter-of-factly, "Because you wouldn't wake up. We wanted you to come out onto the battlefield and talk to us."

Michael still couldn't believe what was happening. He was wide awake. Somehow, he was conversing with soldiers from the battle of Gettysburg one-hundred, thirty-two years ago right in his hotel room. He still couldn't see anyone, yet their presence was quite distinct. The sergeant among them identified the group as members of the 116th Pennsylvania Volunteers.

One soldier inquired, "Is that your missus?" He was referring to Barbara.

But before Michael could respond, another soldier laughingly spoke up, "No, that ain't his missus. They have different last names." This comment brought a chuckle from the group.

The man in charge of the unit apologized for setting off the car alarm, as well as the sounds of the bombardment. "It was the only way we could get your attention to wake you up. It won't happen again." He turned to Virgil, a teenage soldier among them, "Virgil, go stand by the car and guard it the rest of the weekend. Make sure no one bothers it."

Collectively, the group decided it was time for them to leave. Their leader, who the others now referred to as Clem, turned to leave. Over his shoulder he remarked to Michael Flood, "See you later, Johnny."

That same night in Richmond, Virginia, Tim Fredrickson, another Confederate reenactor, had a similar experience within minutes of Michael's. About 3:00 a.m. Tim was sound asleep when he was startled awake by a man's voice. "Wake up! Wake up!" He looked around but couldn't find the person talking. Again, he fell asleep.

Fifteen minutes later Tim heard it again. "Wake up! Wake up! It's time to get up!" He reacted the same way; still he couldn't see anyone in his room. Soon, Tim fell fast asleep.

Then he felt a very cold hand on his shoulder, shaking him gently. The voice said, "Wake up. Wake up. You can't delay any longer!" Tim was jarred to sit bolt upright in bed. No one was in sight in the room.

Barbara and Michael drove to Culp's Hill and Spangler's Spring. They were waiting for the arrival of Nannette and Carolyn Morrison and Tim Fredrickson. Once at Culp's Hill, Michael and Barbara climbed the observation tower to take photos of the countryside. The view was beautiful and the weather was great. But when Barbara attempted to photograph the area towards Devil's Den and the Round Tops, her camera malfunctioned—no focus whatsoever! When she aimed it in all the other directions, it produced photos with no problem. Perplexed at these events they returned to the inn to meet the other three.

As soon as we emerged from the car, Michael and Barbara met us to excitedly recall details of the night before. Each of us was amazed to learn that Tim and Michael had had such similar occurrences so close in time, yet so far apart in distances. Nor had the two men had a previous opportunity to compare stories. Then the five of us dispersed to our separate rooms after making further plans to soon meet at the foot of Devil's Den.

I was in my room barely two minutes when events began to quicken. I removed a jade ring from my finger and placed it on the dresser. My plans were to change into warmer clothes before traipsing around the battlefield; I didn't intend to lose the ring outside. I reached for the dresser with my right hand, Suddenly, the ring slid six inches to the left and disappeared. "Well, that's odd," I thought. "Maybe I bumped something causing it to hit the ring." My intention was to pick it up and put it in a jewelry tray. Confused at where the ring had disappeared to, I picked up my umbrella and purse, the only two items on the dresser. Surely the ring had slid under the purse. But no, it wasn't there.

My gaze shifted to the jewelry tray. There lay the jade ring inside the tray, two feet away and in the opposite direction from which it had slid! Some unseen visitor had placed it there for me, and with a fantastic sleight of hand.

We lost no time getting to Devil's Den. The five of us regrouped there, but each had a direction of his or her own to follow. Barbara had more camera problems in Devil's Den and again later in the Valley of Death. Michael experienced strong energy shifts in each of these areas.

My own mission was to visit the Valley of Death alone. As I picked my way through snow and mud, I was drawn to a cluster of rocks and trees at the base of Devil's Den. Here I sat for several minutes in silent meditation, attempting to glean information on events there either from the past or present. Soon, I could envision Colonel Oates nearby, head bent in sorrow with tears being shed over the loss of his soldiers. We seemed surrounded by several soldiers both Union and Confederate now preparing to leave the battlefield. Church bells rang out from the direction of Gettysburg township. Four other witnesses heard these bells that Saturday morning. Again, we were reminded that there are today no church bells in the town. From his perch atop Devil's Den, Tim Fredrickson watched as I sat in prayer and meditation. For three minutes, Tim watched as I vanished from sight, then reappeared. My mission complete, I rejoined the group near Devil's Den.

The others were ready to move on. Once in our vehicles we drove around the loop above Devil's Den. Michael and Barbara were in their car ahead. Suddenly, they slammed on their brakes. Michael had driven by these monuments many times, but never before had he noticed the regiment on one in particular. It was the 116th Pa. Volunteers' monument.

Following Michael's lead, everyone parked their cars and walked across the road. Michael was compelled to get a closer look at the face of the man lying down as part of the monument. The face was that of a very young man, no beard or mustache. The energy around the monument felt electrical.

Later that same evening, we gathered to decide on our dinner arrangements. Tim suggested half-jokingly to Michael that we all visit the battlefield at dark after dinner. "No way! I've had enough of this spooky stuff! After dinner Barbara and I are going to sit in the hotel lobby and mind our own business," Michael was emphatic.

This too would change. Over dinner we briefly rehashed the day's experiences. Then conversation led to other topics. As the discussion went on, Michael soon seemed quite distracted. He politely interjected a comment on what he was experiencing. "I'm seeing a vivid scene in the field just beyond the 116th monument. It's a clear day with green grass and leaves on the trees. There's no one standing. I see bodies of soldiers strewn all over the field." Suddenly, Michael received a strong, distant message. "We are being summoned to go to that field—**NOW**! We have to pay the bill and go directly." It was 7:55 p.m.

Barbara led the expedition alone in her car. Tim and Michael followed. As they drove down Wheatfield Drive toward the monument to the 116th Pennsylvania Volunteers, Barbara caught the impression of a large animal in the headlights of her car. It moved swiftly from the direction of Sickles Avenue and disappeared. Barbara was certain that it was not a deer, but appeared more to be a dog. Whatever she saw unnerved her.

In the rear vehicle Tim also caught a glimpse of the same creature. Only Tim described it as an Irish Wolfhound. He saw it pass in front of Barbara's car and run toward the fence. However, the animal never jumped the fence. If anything, it disappeared through it!

8:30 p.m. The three adventurers emerged from their cars. Barbara had already had enough excitement; she chose to remain by the roadside. Michael and Tim, however, ventured further out into the field behind the 116th Pennsylvania Volunteers monument. The two were instantly bombarded with undeniably strong energy. Although Michael could not physically see anyone present, he had the distinct sensations of many presences. "They were all around us," he says. "I had the feeling that they were walking by us and going further beyond us into the field. I was beginning to feel nervous, not to mention a little scared."

Barbara, still waiting beside the road, became even more ner-

Nannette Morrison

Gettysburg—February, 1995 in the Triangular Field. Soldier leaning over rock wall overlooking Devil's Den (between 1st and 2nd trees on left).

vous. She began having sharp pains in her chest. She also became frightened yet was intrigued by the scenario.

Tim who was closer to the monument was also experiencing electrical charges in the atmosphere. He glanced at Michael. What he saw startled him. Michael was frozen in a crouched position similar to that of a sprinter at the starting block. He stared out toward the wide open field. "Tim, do you see them?!" Michael can't remember whether he yelled it or whispered.

Soldiers were popping up out of the ground, more and more of them standing in silent, perfect formations of companies. In minutes which seemed like hours, three distinct groups had aligned in perfect files and rows—a whole regiment! Their unearthly figures were darkly silhouetted against the February night's sky. The regimental colors stood furled and out at the front of the regiment. "It was too dark to see facial features, but I knew they were all looking directly at us. I didn't feel threatened by them. We knew they weren't there to harm us." Michael says.

Tim witnessed exactly the same scene. "I saw three company-sized formations, not more than fifty yards in front of us. The whole thing reminded me of the scene in the movie, '*Jason and the Argonaunts*' when the skeletons are rising out of the ground. Two companies were in front with one company in back, about one hundred forty to one hundred sixty men," he describes the scene. "While the companies formed, a horseman appeared from behind the footsoldiers. The horse and rider stopped about twenty-five yards from us. Even though we still couldn't see facial features, I am convinced that it was Colonel St. Clair Mulholland, the commander of the 116th Pennsylvania Volunteers at Gettysburg."

Michael began backing slowly out of his 'sprint' position. "Tim, they're staring right at us! Why are they staring at us?" Michael wondered. He was fascinated and scared simultaneously.

"I think it's time to leave," declared Tim. It took no convincing to get Michael's agreement. As they returned to the cars, Barbara was having difficulty breathing. She never saw the soldiers appear, but she was certain that the others had. During the time they were out in the field, Barbara kept having the feeling of being watched from the woods across the field. Michael finally became aware of the physical discomforts his body had been undergoing due to the surrounding energies. This tremendously powerful energy still lingered as the trio departed.

It would not be until the following day that any of those three people became familiar with the history of the 116th Pennsylvania Volunteers. The morning of the July 2, 1863 in Gettysburg the 116th mustered only one hundred forty-two men on their roles because of previous losses. The unit had not been replenished. At the time of their retreat after fighting at Gettysburg, their regimental colors had been furled and put to the shoulder, just as Michael saw them the night before. The spot where they suffered their heaviest losses and from where they chose to retreat was the same location that those three people had witnessed such drama that Saturday night.

Back in the lobby of the hotel, they regrouped to warm themselves in front of the fire. Barbara smelled it first—the distinct odor of pipe tobacco. Yet, no one was in sight nor had there been anyone around smoking all evening according to Sandy, the desk clerk. At first the tobacco scent was situated in front of the gas fireplace. Shortly, it relocated near a couch out of the way of the fireplace. Michael then had a sense that it was an "older" soldier sitting on the sofa smoking his pipe. The group soon tired from the day's activities and went to their respective rooms.

Michael wasted no time falling asleep. Barbara, however, opted to read several chapters in a book. After this she went into the bathroom. The first thing she noticed as she returned was her crushed pack of cigarettes lying on the bed. Her lighter had disappeared!

"What's wrong? What are you doing?" Michael wondered.

Barbara was thrashing about the bed, tearing it apart. "Somebody crushed my cigarettes and took my lighter. Don't you mess with me Michael!" She was very upset and angry.

He assured her that he wasn't the culprit. Together, they searched the bed and surrounding area thoroughly. Barbara was adamant, "I had the cigarettes and the lighter on the night stand. I came back from the bathroom, and this is what happened!"

Ten minutes had passed since Michael was awakened. He said, "Okay, let's look again. It has to be here." The two of them went over the bed once more. Suddenly, the lighter reappeared just barely under the blanket.

"Don't you dare mess with me, Michael!" Barbara warned him. Eventually, they got to sleep again.

3:33 a.m. Michael was jarred wide awake. "Artillery!" he yelled while running to the window. Barbara was also awake for this excitement. However brief, there had been sounds of firing around Gettysburg.

3:00 a.m. Tim was awakened by a loud knock on his hotel door. The knock wasn't repeated, so he rolled over, slipping back into slumber.

3:12 a.m. Tim felt a heavy nudge on his shoulder. He woke up and stared straight into the face of a Union sergeant! There were four other men in the room with them—a corporal and three privates. Quite politely, the sergeant asked if they could come into his room.

"You're already here! Now, you're asking if it's okay for you to come in?" Tim responded with an amused yet incredulous expression.

The sergeant laughed back at him in the midst of politely apologizing for the intrusion. "We simply want to know why all of you have come to Gettysburg?" At the same time, three of the men pulled out little silver flasks and offered Tim something to drink from a tin cup. Tim then learned the sergeant's name was Thomas Callahan.

"Where's Virgil?" Tim inquired about the youngest soldier. "I would like to speak to him too."

They indicated that he was outside pulling picket duty. One private left, then immediately returned with Virgil. It seems that the teenager was the regiment's go-fer. The men remained with Tim until about 6:00 a.m. At this time Virgil announced abruptly to everyone, "I have to go." And he left. The other men stayed until 6:30 a.m.

6:00 a.m. Michael Flood is awakened by Virgil walking into his room. He politely spoke to Michael, "I played some games with the two of you earlier in the morning. I took it to keep warm and to have a souvenir. I saw how mad Barbara was, so I returned it. You know you have a real fiery-tempered woman there." At this remark they both laughed. Virgil continued his explanation. "I am the youngest member of the 116th Pennsylvania Volunteers, and I am sixteen years old. I have been guarding your car as I was ordered, but it's awfully cold out there. I'm really not a thief; I didn't mean to steal the lighter." The boy's demeanor changed, "Please tell everyone 'good-bye' for me. It's my time and now I am leaving."

Michael suggested that Virgil go toward the bright light and that the warmth there would help guide him. Only later was Michael to realize what he'd said.

Yet, Virgil seemed to already know that was where he was headed. At 6:20 a.m. Virgil was finally gone.

The next day Sunday at Gettysburg was "blue" cold—zero degrees with a high wind chill factor making it twenty below. Needless to say, our excursion onto the battlefield was hasty. Most of our touring was accomplished from the car. However, I had a few shots remaining on my camera, and I was determined to use the film. Not long into the day, our group said their "farewells" to begin the journey home. We departed to leave the Gettysburg ghosts behind. Or, so it would seem.

Monday at 6:00 p.m. Sandy the desk clerk from the inn, called Michael in New York. She was alone on duty at the front desk. Her attention was focused on work at the computer. Some distinct shift in energy behind her caused the woman to turn around. Suspended approximately four feet over the registration desk, hung a glowing whitish-blue thick haze. A sweet, fruity odor accompanied the apparition. As Sandy describes, "The whole experience only lasted ten or fifteen seconds, but sometimes even that can seem like forever!"

The spirits at Gettysburg are very much alive and real.

Nannette Morrison

Gettysburg— February, 1995 in the Slaughter Pen. Soldiers face (above left arrow) and wagon wheel (above right arrow).

Shadow of Death

Of all the research and work accomplished for *Echoes of Valor*, as well as *A Thundering Silence*, countless incidents were astonishing. One taped meditation produced the rhythmic tapping cadence of a drummer boy practicing his keys on the rim of a drum. Nearly all provide evidence that, not only are the spirits among us, but that it is possible to assist them to a higher spiritual level. This meditation session with Tim Fredrickson, a reenactor with the 5th Virginia Infantry Regiment, on August 14, 1994 was no exception.

Tim's voice began softly, drifting through the ethers, "...wonderful floating feeling. Lots of travel...through every dimension...not alone, definitely not alone. Others all around. They're not confined to our concept of time, from all 'time periods.' Sensation of flying like in a hang glider, free and loose. Lots of beautiful colors! Free-fall feeling, but there is a destination up ahead." As he described the experiences, he was completely unaware of the erratic tapping motion of his right hand.

I gently reminded him, "Don't worry about trying to figure out what's happening. Let the energy flow, and let's just make it known to the energy source, the Universal energy, that neither one of us logically 'know' how to interpret these letters or notes or whatever it they may be. Ask if there is something that we're supposed to be aware of, or if it can be offered to us in a way that we might be able to understand it and benefit from it. See if that's appropriate."

"This is the really odd part," Tim objectively observed. "I feel as though I'm standing next to a telephone pole or telegraph pole with my ear against it, and I'm feeling the vibrations."

"That sounds like fun," I couldn't resist kidding.

Tim laughed, "Yeah, that's a lot of fun, just what you ought to do on a Sunday afternoon. Go stand next to a telegraph pole, which doesn't exist anymore, and listen to the clicking sound. Now I know I'm going down to Malvern Hill or Cold Harbor some afternoon, and I'll find a telephone pole. The little guys in the white coats are gonna come get me because they'd heard that some guy was standing around listening to the base of phone poles!"

"Keep breathing deeply," I reminded him. "Let's imagine that that telegraph pole is here now. See what the information is, and we're not linearly or logically attempting to figure out what the message is. Ask the sender,...let's ask the Universe for permission to know what's being put out there. See if we can 'tap' into it. See who is on the sending end—a face or impression. Who's sending the message, and what are they trying to tell us, and maybe 'why' as well?"

"Real strong vibrations...like a wave...," the almost distant voice continued.

At this space on the audio tape, what distinctly sounds like an extra "heartbeat," that of a third person not visibly present in the room, is recorded. For four distinct minutes at the end of one side and continuing on to the other side of the cassette, is the rhythmic beat of a heart.

Tim's voice picked up here. "May, the month of May, 1865...early May ... just when I'm ...," he faded out.

Encouragement was needed for him to proceed. "So, what is the significance of May, 1865? What do we need to know about that date?"

"I am floating above a city that has to be Richmond. I can basically see the entire series of defense works around the city. I can see the James (River), see Drewery's Bluff ... the entire line of defenses almost stretching ... I see down to Petersburg," he spoke slowly.

"Why are you being shown that now?" I asked.

"I don't know. There's a definite, very strong energy coming from the whole city. I can't locate a particular locale. It's definitely Richmond though. I'm high enough that I can go all the way down to Petersburg with my sight, if you want to call it sight. Oh, I see Cold harbor, but it's not Cold Harbor. Oh man ... I can feel ... this is real different ... I can feel the run of emotions coming off of the city of Richmond now. I guess because you can say it's one of the most troubled times in the history of the city."

I didn't wish for Tim to force information. "Don't struggle with it; don't attempt to figure it out. Let the energy flow smoothly and go with the experience. Allow yourself to be there and to see what you need to see there."

"There's a sense of foreboding, almost like everyone knows (that) as much as they wasn't to hold the defense line around Richmond, they almost know the fall of Richmond is inevitable. It's a sense of deep frustration. There's that deep belief , that really strong emotion of a belief in a cause that's still there. But that ...I don't want to call it a foreboding, it's not exactly a foreboding ... it's just that they know ... everybody knows that the odds are against them in this point in time," his voice sounded nearly confused at so much information and emotion at once.

"So let's maintain the breathing. Focus on your body, breathing deeply," I reminded him.

"That telegraphing ... I know what it is now. It's not like I've been able to understand the messages. They're coming in from every point in the Confederacy. And, it's the messages of every day of setbacks ... of either minor fights, minor battles that could have been victories, that have turned into defeats, or even minor victories that only amount to nothing because all they are seemingly a finger in that proverbial dike of overwhelming odds against the Confederacy. The little kid is not a Dutch boy. It's a little sixteen-year-old Confederate soldier sticking his finger in a hole." Tim paused shortly to laugh. "... Sticking his finger in a hole in a dike trying to hold back this wall of water, but he's the only thing that's holding it back. He symbolizes a minor victory," he laughed again at the image. "But that's what's causing the frustration; it's like a noose around you that's being drawn tighter and tighter. You're doing what you can to get rid of it. You want to but you know it's inevitable."

"Keep breathing deeply and evenly," I said.

He continued, "There's a really strong ... I'm trying to home in on it. There's one point that's really stronger than the others ... got it! Got it! I can see it now ... a series of earthworks, very clearly earthworks. They seem to be very sparsely defended, as if they know .... Well, it's not as if they know; it's all they have to put in this area. They're all very young and very old. I guess you could say it's the bottom of the barrel. I'm looking at two miles, a rough estimate of the length of the area I'm scanning on. I'd say it's about two miles of earthworks and defense works. There can't be more than six hundred men defending the entire section of earthworks."

"Breathe, Tim." It's so easy to get caught up in talking that the entire experience can be lost."

"Six hundred men to defend two miles ... I think on a rough estimate, very rough ... that's probably ten men for every two hundred feet. I can feel a lot of pain, a lot of suffering. The reason I believe that is, these men really are the bottom of the barrel. A lot of them are walking wounded, convalescents from the hospitals. They've been pulled out basically because they can walk and fire a rifle. They've been put into units so badly depleted through desertions or casualties that there's nobody else to fill the holes. Even then there's not enough to fill the holes. They're a bare, bare ration."

I interrupted briefly, "Where do you think this is. What are you looking at?"

"There's road ...there's a road that comes ...I can tell, through the center of Richmond. It goes right up to the earthworks, and the earthworks break the road. It's moved to the left ...obviously what was a main road, not necessarily gravel, but a main dirt road. It's on the west end of the defenses, and it seems to be on the very far extent of the defenses themselves. I can't really ...I'd say it's out of the city limits, out of the actual city limits of Richmond. Somewhere ...somewhere, I think in Henrico County, defenses on the west side. I'm being drawn ... there's really a very strong wave or barrage of energy, of electricity coming from one particular spot. I'm trying to home in on that spot."

"Relax and breathe," I reminded him.

Tim attempted further description, "Something, something ... field ... something field. I can see 'em now."

"See who?" I wondered.

"I can see ... well they call themselves a company but there's no more than eighteen ... eighteen men altogether assigned to a section of these defenses. They don't have really any unity. When I say a company, they don't have a designation other than that they're assigned to defend this section of the defenses," he replied.

"So why are we being shown this now?" I asked. "What can we do about it ...if anything?"

"There's a very strong energy coming not from the entire group," Tim continued. "But coming from a number of them ... because I don't .... No, no there was actual fighting. There was no combat in this sector of the defenses, but there were men who died here.... There were men who did not leave this area. And I can see the entire group of eighteen to twenty, just sitting there in the shelters they've built in the trenches. There's a real sadness to them though. It's like they know that some of them are not going to leave this area, this 'spot,' this very spot! It's not like there's a battle eminent! But it's like some of us are going to stay here."

"What can we do about that?" I interjected. "What can we do about the ones that are going to be left? Any faces, names, personal information at all on them?"

"Oh...this is odd, very, very odd!" Tim exclaimed.

"Explain what's odd." My curiosity had intensified.

Tim, still lying down and 'tuning in' to the circumstances, studied the situation a bit before going on. "It's like I'm looking at, ... if it ever existed, a group photo of these men. But it's like somebody took the photo, and there's shadow, a distinct shadow hanging over members of that group."

"Which ones have that shadow over them?" I asked.

"I can see two standing, er ... kneeling. It's like a group photo. Nine of 'em are standing and another eight or nine are kneeling in the front as if they're being photographed. And, there's a really strong shadow over two in particular in the front row .... then another one, two, three, four, in the back row, six altogether. One of them in the front row is gaunt, very emaciated. Kendall, I don't know if it's a first or last name. Kendall is very strong," He assured me.

Then I asked him, "Who's beside Kendall?"

"The other one with the shadow ... with the shadow above him is about three people down from him, Tim explained. "He's quite young, almost ... I want to say 'too young to be with these guys' but I know better."

"Does that one have a name?" Again, I urged him for more details.

"Bradley ... Bradley," he responded tentatively. "I don't know if it's a first or last name. I can't figure it out."

I reminded him, "Breathe deeply. Don't try to 'figure it out'."

Tim still struggled with the name. "Bradley! I *know* these two! I don't know why ... don't know why."

"Does this photograph actually exist now?" I inquired.

"No, no it's shown in my view as if it's a photograph, but this never existed as a photo as we know of one ... or even as we'd take it!" Tim was quite excited at the scene, as well as agitated. "It's as if I'm seeing them, but I don't know that this ever took place!"

"Who else is there in that photo?" I encouraged him.

He attempted to go into further detail. "This is ... I *know* these two in front. It's there, that black shadow or aura is hanging above them."

I waited patiently, then asked, "Where have you seen them before? Ask *them* so that you are not using the logical facets of your brain. Allow the intuitive side to function properly."

Tim's body tensed dramatically here. "Oh my gosh! Oh, no! It's the two! Oh man, oh man, I know where I am! The road ... the Richmond—Louisa, Louisa Courthouse Turnpike Road. I don't know what it was really called. But I'm standing basically on what is now route 250 on the outskirts of Richmond. It's clearer now!" He was excited at the recognition. "if it's the two soldiers I've been seeing standing there by the road! It's as clear as a bell! That's why they're so familiar."

"Sure. Ask Kendall and Bradley to speak distinctly, clearly to see what information they can give us."

"Damn it! Why didn't that come to me before?" Tim sounded impatient.

Tim, you're blocking the energy flow. Focus on the two of them, as opposed to the logic," I reminded him.

"Weakness, fatigue...," he trailed off in a faint voice.

"Ask if they are willing to move on. Ask if they can go up *the twenty-seven steps* now. See if it's appropriate to do this."

He began slowly, "I can see both of them, and I can see three others. The others have gone... gone from my field of vision completely. Between mid-to-late April to early May, eighteen to twenty men that were assigned to defend this God-forsaken section of the Richmond defenses... Five of them died, not from wounds, not from fighting, just from starvation and disease."

"See if it's time to help them go. Maybe a 'yes,' maybe a 'no'." I urged on for an answer.

"Yes, it is," he was adamant. "They're ready."

I reminded him of the process, one of many similar used by various civilization throughout the ages. "Show them *the twenty-seven steps*—if that's even necessary. The important thing is to guide them toward that bright light high up. We have a lot of protection where we are to do this work."

"Maxwell... Hillman... Jacobs... the other three. I can see all five as clear as if they were standing right in front of me now on this spot."

My inclination was to keep the focus on track. "Let them see that bright, white light directly above them. Assure them that it is okay to move on."

"They're going... one by one, they're going. They can feel the burden being lifted from them as if they're just being lifted off the ground from that very spot. They're going right up. It's like a tunnel this time! I know it's the *proverbial twenty-seven steps*, but it's like a golden tunnel. And they're being lifted right off the ground!" Tim was amazed at the sight.

"So what do you see at the top, if anything, as they go up?"

"Somebody is waiting for them! I can't see him; yet I have a sense of a *Presence*. It's a *Presence*, a very benevolent and guiding *Presence*. And He's bringing them up to where they belong! One, two , three, four , five... they're all gone!" He seemed in awe at the experience.

I wished to give him ample time to move the energy before I encouraged him to continue.

"I can't see them; I know that their energy is still around me though. They're still right here, in a way. I can sense them, yet they're not really here. That sounds awful! They're here and not here either!" Tim was perplexed.

"No, it isn't awful," I assured him. "They've been on this level a long time."

Tim was still feeling the results of the experience. "I can feel their pain and their emotions. It's washed over me, but it was different this time. I was like a rock on a shore. As each one left, as each one was gone, I knew it was washing over me. I could feel it being expelled! Totally expelled from their bodies, minds and souls — everything that they had suffered. Yet, it wasn't like it was going into me this time. It was like that rock on a shore, and it just washed over me. It passed over and retreated and then was gone, ebbed away. But, I felt it... really, really felt it—not in the same manner."

An explanation was in order for Tim. "We had changed your vibrations high enough that you wouldn't feel their pain. We'd asked permission to go up one notch higher so that you physically wouldn't feel their discomfort. That's not necessary in order to do this work."

"Each one... I knew who he was, yet I didn't. I knew everything about him. I could see and feel both sides, the open side... as well as the dark side that you can't see. All five of them when they went up, released it all to me, through me, but past me at the same time. Past me as if it was solid and broke against that rock. And, by breaking against the rock, everything went to where it was supposed to be. It seemed order, not chaos. Like a shattered mirror, it broke into a thousand pieces, but each one is aligned like a dividing line down the middle. Organized chaos... and there was a catalyst, a reason for it."

"You're starting to hold your breath again," I observed. "So many words inhibit the Life Force experience, consequently the energy flow. Gradually ease yourself back."

Men of War

On September 18, 1963 from Camp Fort Spring, Greenbrier County, Virginia, James P. Peck wrote this letter to his Aunt and Uncle Snidow.

"I this evening seat myself to write you a letter for the first one since I have been on service but you must excuse me this time and I will try and write oftener. I am well at present[1] and hope this may find you in good health.

"There was something mysterious seen near Lewisburg and at different places in the county. I will give you the particulars. On Tuesday the 1st of this month Mr. Dwyer, a gentleman residing near the Kanawha Turnpike happened to be at a neighbors (Mr. Piercy) sitting on the porch with Mr. Piercy's family when one of them called his attention to a body of mysterious rectangular objects moving vertically through the air just above the trees in an adjacent sugar orchard. These objects were apparently about eight feet long, two and a half in width and one inch thick. They were white tinged a little with green. They moved directly north in a column about fifty yards wide with the order and regularity of soldiers. The rear was nearer the ground than the front and consequently had to pass through the orchard. In emerging from the trees they resumed their original order and so remained until out of sight.

"Immediately following but a little further west was seen a vast army of men dressed in white and moving in quick time and in as good order as soldiers on dress parade. After passing any obstacle they would resume their places in ranks. Thus passed the entire column occupying more than an hour and presenting a scene of awful grandeur and sublimity to those who beheld it. Whether this be a dream, an optical delusion [sic], or means used by Omnipotence to foreshadow events and to strengthen his suffering people, I will not endeavor to determine. I will state however, that those who know the parties well, give them credit for candor, intelligence, and veracity."

This account and the one which follows are recorded for history in the Civil War Annals. It is recorded in *Hard Times 1861-1865*, Vol. I. This is as Mr. Moses Dwyer described it immediately after the event.

"A remarkable phenomenon was witnessed a few miles west of Lewisburg, Greenbrier Co. Virginia (now West Virginia) on the 1st of October, 1863, about 3:00 P.M., by Mr. Moses Dwyer, who happened to be seated on his porch at the time, as well as by others at or near the house.

"The weather was quite hot and dry; not a cloud could be seen; no wind even ruffled the foliage on the surrounding trees. All things being propitious, the grand panorama began to move. Just over and through the tops of the trees on the adjacent hills, to the south, immense numbers of rolls, resembling cotton or smoke, apparently of the size and shape of doors, seemed to be passing rapidly through the air, yet in beautiful order and regularity. The rolls seemed to be tinged on the edge with light green, so as to resemble a border of deep fringe. There were apparently thousands of them; they were perhaps an hour in getting by. After they had passed over and out of sight, the scene was changed from the air above to the earth beneath, and became more intensely interesting to the spectators who were witnessing the panorama from different stand-points.

"In the deep valley beneath, thousands upon thousands of (apparently) human beings (men) came in view; travelling in the same direction as the rolls, marching in good order, some thirty or forty in depth, moving rapidly—'double-quick'—and commenced ascending the almost insurmountable hills opposite, and had the stoop peculiar to men ascending a steep mountain. There seemed to be a great variety in the size of the men; some were very large, whilst others were quite small. Their arms, legs, and heads could be distinctly seen in motion. They seemed to observe strict military discipline, and there were no stragglers.

"There was uniformity of dress; white blouses or shirts, with white pants; they were without guns, swords, or anything that indicated 'men of war.' On they came through the valley and over the steep road, and finally passing out of sight, in a direction due north from those who were looking on.

"Four others (respectable ladies) and a servant girl witnessed this strange phenomenon. On the 14th instant the same scene, almost identical, was seen by eight or ten of the Confederate pickets at Runger's Mill, and by many of the citizens in that neighborhood; this is about four miles west of Percy's. It was about an hour passing.

[1] James Polk Peck, son of John Snidow Peck and Mary Burk Snidow, would be killed later on June 3, 1864 at Gaines Mill, Chickahominy River.

Footprints

Today, George and Micheline Paris live in the old brick tavern at Charlotte Courthouse, Virginia. Their home has been comfortable and quite calm since they moved in July, 1994. This wasn't always the situation, however. Particularly during its restoration, the old tavern showed signs of an active spiritual life.

Built in 1820 the tavern remained such for nearly one hundred years. One prominent innkeeper was Wyatt Cardwell who ran the tavern until the Civil War erupted. Following its public use, the structure became a private home. The former tavern became a private school in 1967. Eventually, the school went out of business, at which time the Parises purchased the building. George and Micheline began restoring the old tavern back to its original design.

One afternoon George commented to a friend who was helping him complete some plastering, "I wonder what Wyatt Cardwell would think of the place now since it's looking again like a tavern instead of a school?"

Just then all the bells which had not yet been disconnected, went off ringing in a frenzy. George went to the main switch which controlled the bells. It didn't work. He then went to the electric box to turn off the circuits leading to the bells. Yet, when he turned the circuit back on, the bells did not resume.

The men had a good laugh over the incident. Andrew said, "Well, I guess he likes the idea!"

George wasn't so sure. "Gee, I don't know what he thinks. He just rang the bells. Maybe he hates it."

On another occasion Andrew had gone alone to the tavern to continue plastering. As soon as George arrived, Andrew called to him, "Come here. I want to show you something. All the doors were locked when I got here, exactly as I left them last night." He was pointing down at a trail in the plaster dust from the previous day.

Clearly they could see two sets of footprints — one of a small child and one of a man — beginning from nowhere but leading into the bedroom. There they stopped abruptly. "It was very mysterious," says Mr. Paris. "We couldn't figure who or why or how anyone could be in there since it was locked all around.

The Parises also talk about a particular door into the dining room. Every time Andrew and George left the tavern, they would close the door securely. But each time they returned, it was open.

"It was especially mysterious," explains George, "because the door didn't naturally swing open in that direction. We tested it several times to see if it was a matter of the building settling on its own. But no. In fact, the door would only open on its own at night after we had locked up and departed.

House of Spirits

The powerful strains of Tchaikovsky's "Concerto No. 1 in B flat minor" filled the front parlor. Flawlessly, effortlessly, Eva's fingers glided over the keyboard. Even with her eyes closed and no music in front of her, she played the complicated piano piece, introduced in Boston in 1875, as if she had done so hundreds of times. In fact, Eva had done just that, as well as Tchaikovsky's overture to "Romeo and Juliet" (1869) and nearly all of his works.

Eva reconstructed the notes of music from the depths of her heart and mind, the source of her book on the symphonic composer's life. Even though she'd never met "in the flesh", nor had she read anything about him, the elderly woman had authored a perfectly accurate first-person account of Tchaikovsky's life. Similarly, Eva had never read his music. In actuality, she'd only taken three music lessons in her life. Yet the compositions flowed remarkably through her fingers.

The woman at the piano smiled demurely. She "knew" the man alright.... Oh yes, how well she "knew" the man! Eva had been in communication with Tchaikovsky by channeling his Spirit for twenty years. Still, the energy of this man was only one of the many among her House of Spirits.

Jeremy stood staring anxiously at the house built at the turn of the century. This would be his first visit inside the house since he was a young man. His grandmother Eva had 'passed away' last winter, that of 1992. Now it was left to him to make repairs and renovations for tenants. Cautiously, he walked toward the front door, finally taking hold of the doorknob. Nothing stood between him and the house to which he'd vowed adamantly never to return.

He entered the front hallway... nothing happened. Jeremy toured from room to room. The house was stripped of furnishings, yet he began to have flashes of memories in every room. He'd always been a little afraid of his Grandma Eva. Her uncanny way of sneaking around then scaring him kept him on edge. She could enter a room soundlessly, nearly motionless. Eva especially delighted in relocating instantly in a room while Jeremy briefly looked away.

The staircase to the second floor lay before him. He was aware that he needed to see her bedroom, the room in which she had died. Jeremy made the climb, then turned the corner to enter Eva's room. The single remaining piece of furniture was her prized oak Victorian bureau. Jeremy was to transport it to his home in Maryland. He opened each empty drawer. Then he pulled out the last one. The items lying within gave him goose bumps. A Ouija board, boxes of matches and wax candles, tarot cards, numerous channeling paraphernalia, assorted books on transmediumship and transmigration remained for him to dispose of.

Spontaneously, he recalled his last visit with his grandmother. An amateur photographer, Jeremy was summoned to photograph paintings ready for shipment to a national gallery. He arranged the equipment in the back sunroom for maximum lighting. His tripod was situated in the center of the room. So far all had gone well individually photographing the art work.

As he positioned the last painting on the easel across from the camera, Eva silently left the room. Jeremy held his eye to the lens and adjusted it. The picture went out of focus. Again he corrected the lens. Before he could snap the shutter, the painting seemed to shift to one side! Frustrated and bewildered, Jeremy took his face away from the tripod and camera. The painting was suspended in midair in front of the camera; nothing and no one was touching it!

That was the final straw for the young man. "Grandmother! Where are you? Come quickly!" he beseeched her.

Eva glided silently into the sunroom with that innocent look of hers. "What is it, Dear? What could possibly create such a stir?"

He turned pointing toward the mysterious canvas. It was back securely resting on its easel. "That picture was floating around the room by itself!" Jeremy yelled. As quickly as he could pack the equipment, he was out of there.

Later in the afternoon of his return, Jeremy unloaded his van packed with supplies. Electrical wiring was required in addition to painting and cleaning windows. His two cats, Ming and Tao, who frequently traveled with him wanted out of the vehicle. Jeremy carried each to the front door, releasing them inside. Ming, however, seemed especially unhappy. She sank two sets of claws into his shoulder before he could get her loose. Both cats were instantly nervous.

Electrical work was first on his list. Jeremy set to the task right away. He intended to accomplish as much as possible before darkness set in. The work flowed smoothly as he listened to a radio he'd carried along. At times he felt Eva's presence, like eyes were observing his every move. Then as the shadows of evening advanced through the windows, he established a stopping point.

"Okay Ming and Tao, you'll have to stay here tonight. The hotel won't allow you in my room." Jeremy assured the cats that they'd be fine until morning. In his gut he felt a pang of guilt; nobody could pay him enough money to stay there overnight alone.

Jeremy returned to the house after breakfast. When he opened the kitchen door to greet his cats, they acted terrified. Both of them screamed and hissed while ridges of hair stood up on their spines. Never had he seen either animal in such a state of fright, ready to fight. Their food and water had not been touched all night. They acted more like caged tigers than calm domestic seasoned travelers. Finally, he was able to catch them and take them out to the van where they remained for the extent of his stay.

Insulation had to be installed today. Jeremy busied himself tearing out paneling, then banging and hammering to get the job done. With his athletic 6'5" frame, he was prepared for heavy labor. Again he felt the presence of others around him. It was a thick, dismal feeling. In abject frustration Jeremy discovered himself talking to the house asking it to, "Leave me alone and let me get this done."

The response was sounds of children's laughter somewhere near him. The voices had a peculiar bouncing echo to them. "Now I'm hearing things!" he declared to himself. Closer than before, the youthful laughter of several children surrounded him. Jeremy dropped the hammer. "What do you want from me?" He stepped toward the voices.

Several yards further toward the stairway, he heard them again. They reminded him of children playing in a tunnel. Scared as he was, Jeremy was compelled to follow their sounds. He wondered how many there were. The laughter faded in and out as it continued to travel. He was being led upstairs; they seemed to barely stay one room ahead of him

All five rooms upstairs were void of occupants. Jeremy searched each one twice. Still the children laughed, mocking him. Suddenly, he'd had enough of their games.

As he started down the stairway, a sense of loathing hit him. Yet before he could react, something invisible tried to choke him! He reeled backward against the wall. Quickly he regained his balance and fled down the hall. One corner of the house had a substantial drain spout attached to the outside. Jeremy struggled with the window closest to the pipe. He jerked it open and slid down the drain spout... anything to escape whatever waited on the stairs.

This was Ralph's second summer house-sitting for his friend. The stone cottage was familiar to him and quite homey. It sat in a little group of trees behind the main house. Before Michael left Charlottesville for California, he mentioned to Ralph that the deceased owner's grandson was expected to show up and make renovations.

When Ralph drove into the circular driveway, he noticed the van parked beside the back door. He decided to walk over and introduce himself. Ralph discovered the man unraveling insulation out back. "Hi there! I'm taking care of my buddy's home for two weeks while he's away."

"Nice to meet you. I'm Mrs. Turner's grandson," the man greeted Ralph amiably. The two men struck an instant friendship, and the conversation quickly rolled around to Eva Turner. "Would you like to see inside? I've got plenty of work to do around here, but you're welcome to see the place."

Ralph was more then mildly curious. The outside had an aura that intrigued him. Not only that, there were strange things happening in the cottage at night that bothered him. Possibly the grandson was approachable with some questions. Ralph admired the large stone fireplace in the living room, then walked toward the front areas. Jeremy stayed with him making comments.

"Okay if I look upstairs?" Ralph asked.

"Sure, go ahead. I just need to check on something down here," Jeremy replied. He had no intention of going up those stairs any time soon.

A brief look upstairs was enough for Ralph. The entire time he walked along the hallway, he had prickly goose bumps on his arms. Ralph soon descended joining Jeremy outside, who inquired if everything was comfortable in the cottage.

"Yes, pretty much so," Ralph replied. But his thoughts raced to see if it was okay to tell the truth. Cautiously, he added, "Actually some unusual things are starting to happen at night."

Jeremy encouraged him to continue, "What sort of things?"

"Last night I woke up about 3:00 a.m. to find all the lights turned on in the cottage. I know I'd turned them all off before I retired. But every single light was on again while I slept!" Ralph paused for a reaction from the guy.

Jeremy only nodded his head asking, "What else?"

"Well," Ralph continued, "this went on through the entire night. At least four more times, I wakened to see all the lights turned back on! Finally, I was exasperated. I yelled to whomever was there, 'Alright I'm not playing games anymore! I'm really tired; just leave me alone!' Geeze, I felt like I was ready for the loony bin. But at that point the activity ceased. When I got up this morning, all the lights were off."

Jeremy nodded his head, all the while listening carefully. Then he decided to share his experiences with Ralph. He spared him no details. Everything he could recall from childhood visits with Grandmother Eva, as well as current occurrences.

"One observation I made," Ralph replied, "was that all this commotion began in the cottage after you arrived and started the hammering and sawing. I arrived a week previous to you, and none of this was evident. Somebody in the big house doesn't like what you're doing."

"It does seem that way," agreed Jeremy. "Nevertheless, my wife and I are intent on renting it out."

Ralph recalled another strange afternoon. "A few days ago, I locked both doors previous to entering the shower. Yet when I came out of the bathroom, both doors were wide open. Even the screen door in the back was flapping in the breeze! At times I've actually felt like I was being watched, as if something has moved into the cottage with me."

During the summer of 1994, Ralph was again asked to house-sit for two weeks. Instead of living in the cottage, he opted to check on it daily, watering the plants and retrieving the mail and newspaper. Five guys were living in the main house at that time.

Ralph approached one of them introducing himself, explaining that his friend was out of town. He would be stopping in to see that all was in order. The conversation was conducted in general small talk until the young man altered its direction.

Bill had moved in only a few months prior to this. He was especially interested to learn that Ralph had spent part of two summers there. "Have you ever heard or felt anything out of the ordinary around here?" he queried Ralph. Bill was testing to see how 'safe' it was to comment further.

"Exactly what are you trying to say?" Ralph answered.

"This house is 'really' strange! There are some crazy things going on in there!" Bill looked in the direction of the main house. At this point Ralph sympathized with the guy. He described to him everything that he'd experienced last summer.

"Thank God you're telling me this. I thought I was losing my mind! We've heard random knocking sounds where we can't locate the source. Doors and windows will slam shut or open on their own. It's like somebody's in there with us playing tricks on us!" Bill insisted.

November of that year I met Ralph for the first time. He had learned of my work with *Echoes of Valor* and wished to talk with me about the Turner house. Ralph had no idea whether Bill would still live there, but he encouraged me to meet the present tenants. Two weeks later I found myself doing just that.

Before we even turned into the driveway from the main road, I felt incredible pressure in my head and chest. A sense of uneasiness accompanied by thick energy surrounded me in the car. Elizabeth Pennel who was with me experienced the same. She described it as strong pressure in the third and fourth body chakras (the stomach and heart areas). It became an effort for me to breathe. As Elizabeth parked her car near the house, we mustered up the courage to approach the front door.

A tall youthful gentleman greeted us from the porch as we walked toward the house. "Hi," I spoke directly trying to explain why the two of us appeared on his doorstep. We launched into a friendly discussion which gradually included the house. I quickly learned that Bill had moved out previous to Tom's arrival.

As Tom spoke more freely regarding his own impressions of the house, I requested permission to record his words. "Sure. That's fine with me," he said.'

I instantly produced a cassette recorder and note pad. Both however, felt as though they were yanked from me! The items flew out of my hands toward the porch and landed five feet beyond me. "Gee, maybe someone else doesn't want me to do this," I speculated.

Once I'd recovered my belongings, Tom continued. "I've heard lots of heavy breathing when no one was around. Every morning about 5:00-6:00 a.m. books will fall off the shelves in the library. Then I took my CPR and lifesaving books out of there. That seemed to stop that disturbance. For a while I kept trying to disregard these events, but they're really persistent. I'd get up at 6:00 a.m. to walk my dogs, and there'd be books all over the floor in there. That went on for two weeks!" He paused a few seconds to see if we were reacting negatively.

Reassurance came from Elizabeth and myself that we found him quite believable. I explained to Tom that I had been investigating this type of phenomena for years. "You are not the only person who's had similar experiences here."

"One owner came by to check on the place shortly after I moved in. That's when there were four other guys living here. They're all gone now though. But, anyway she asked who stayed in what rooms. I showed her around," he explained. "I wanted to tell her what was going in on around here, but I didn't know how," said Tom.

"Yes, there are certain people who'll listen and understand about this sort of thing. Others don't want to hear it," I commented.

Tom was relaxing further as he recalled specific details. Recording the encounter seemed like a therapeutic release for him. "Not long after her visit, all the other guys moved out. That left me here alone with... 'whatever'. Three of those roommates are 300 pound defensive backs for the University of Virginia's football team. They'd had enough of this place! They put two deadbolts on the inside of their bedroom doors and were still afraid to sleep at night!" Tom exclaimed. :"Well after everybody else moved out, things got real lively. I started hearing children's laughter throughout the house... only I could never find it. Water seemed to be running in rooms where there isn't any water or in rooms that have faucets but no water turned on for months."

Since I was familiar with the stories of the voices, I asked Tom more about them. He elaborated further, "The kids' voices and laughter were always upstairs, never down here. Sometimes it was so obvious that I turned up the stereo volume to drown them out. I tried so hard to ignore all of these things. Gradually, I thought I was going crazy! I never knew who to talk to about this. Man, am I glad you showed up today. You probably saved my life, or at least my sanity!" Tom seemed genuinely amazed that we were there to listen.

I was torn between describing to him the possibilities of energies within his home and not wanting to further alarm the man. "Are you a religious person? Do you pray or meditate?" I inquired of Tom.

"Some, especially since my brother died," Tom said. "I also began talking to the house. I let it know that it was 'cool' for these spirits to be here. Then I realized how weird that seemed. Anyway, at that point some of the activities subsided. Part of the time though, I still hear pots and pans rattling in the kitchen."

The entire time while Tom spoke I felt like my throat was closing in. The damp icy cold permeated through my winter clothes. This was a very unnatural atmosphere harboring incredibly strong forces!

With each recollection of detail, other suppressed memories emerged. "My two Doberman puppies will freak at things I can't see or hear," Tom explained. "Sometimes if we're walking outside, they'll be calm, then suddenly jump in midair from fright. It happens frequently near that apple tree over there," he pointed in that direction. "It always scares me too! They do the same thing in the house. Both of them will be quiet or asleep and suddenly they get startled by something nearby in the room, whine in fear, then run to cower at my feet," he said.

"A couple of nights recently it was really bad," Tom resumed. "I try to train the dogs to sleep by the fireplace in the living room, especially while I'm here watching television or reading. These two nights in particular the pups, who at nine months of age are nearly grown, were agitated. Instead of lying down, they stared at something in the hallway. I couldn't see it myself. But they definitely focused all senses on that one area. Both of them had their hair standing in ridges on their backs. One became adventurous. He walked toward the hallway but was immediately backed into the corner here, then cowered down low. That dog was terrified! He whimpered like he was being beaten! I was scared too at that point. I walked all around the downstairs... couldn't see a thing."

Tom had more to tell. "One room upstairs was incredibly noisy when I slept in it. That was my bedroom until everyone else split. I was certain at night that someone was in the room with me or in the attic overhead. Anyway, I put a deadbolt on my door, but it didn't help. I kept my gun loaded and ready to use it. I could hear footsteps in the dark coming toward me across the room. I tried to tell myself that it was only the old house settling. I didn't believe it though. When they weren't walking in my room, I heard them downstairs. Man, I could hardly sleep at all!" he exclaimed.

Again I assured him that others had described to me the same stories about this formidable house of spirits. It was obvious that he'd needed to share these experiences for a long time and to be understood.

"I've had friends come to visit me who would stay in the car. Two of these girls would get as close as the corner of the house, then freeze with chill bumps! At first I thought they were joking, but that's not so. These people are serious! Something unseen prevents them from coming into the house. One friend can't even get out of the car in the driveway there," he insisted.

"There's another aspect of this place that bothers me," Tom said. "the electrical currents are strange. My television and stereo will fade out and in. The lights will dim or flicker dramatically, then brighten, go off, and come back on by themselves. I even have surge protectors on my stereo equipment; but they don't do a bit of good."

Elizabeth was still curious about the sounds of water. "Do you actually find it running or only hear it?" she inquired.

He said, "I've not seen it running, just heard it. The sounds of water began in the kitchen and bathroom down here. Then last week it shifted to the upstairs. Every time I go up there to check the toilet and sink, nothing is running. In fact I turned off the water line leading to the upstairs. It was getting on my nerves.

Tom continued along the vein of the power fluctuations. "A few nights ago some friends came over from Richmond. The television went crazy while they visited. Next we could hear windows slamming upstairs. I hadn't opened any windows in two months, still this was three or four windows slamming shut!" He shook his head like he could hardly believe it all. "The storms are consistently violent around this property, too," Tom explained. "Lightning strikes a tree here nearly every time a storm passes through. I commented on that to one of my roommates when I first arrived. He'd noticed it too. The woodpile has been hit three times this summer. Several trees have dropped across the driveway so that it takes days to get in out of here. I can drive half a mile down the road, and the same storm will be much less intense than here. Eventually I learned that Mrs. Turner had five of six lightning rods attached to the trees out front. Man, you ought to see the lightning bounce around through those trees!

"About two weeks after I'd moved in, the other owners called me long distance. They wanted to come see the inside of the house. It wasn't convenient for me at the time; still they insisted that there was something specific which they had to check on. As soon as the couple arrived, all Hell broke loose! As they stood in the kitchen, all three windows in there slammed shut. I keep sturdy sticks in them to prop them open. That didn't matter; each of the three sticks flew out! The woman turned to her husband and made a stupid remark like, 'Yep— there goes those windows again. Time to go.'" Tom had observed the scene as bizarre. "Whatever was so important for them to check on was forgotten. They didn't stay five minutes."

"Yes, it sounds like they had a change of heart after their arrival," I commented. Telling Tom further of what I knew of the house was important. While doing so I still omitted the most dramatic incidents. He'd already experienced enough to scare any brave soul away.

However, he proceeded with the drama of a physical nature. "Other sensations have increased this week, things I'd not felt previously. Two nights ago I was covering the pool table in the library. Suddenly, I felt a gentle touch between my shoulder blades. I turned quickly, expecting to see something behind me! Nothing was there. Other evenings lately I've felt like someone was touching my neck and shoulders... like fingers crawling on me. Sometimes it's similar to a cool breeze with pressure, yet enough to move my hair. The sounds of heavy breathing have increased again too, especially late at night when I'm watching television. These are like a heavy sigh. I've even heard it outside on the front porch," Tom concluded his stories.

I suggested that he begin a journal of these events. From past investigations I had learned that the psychic activity could increase or decrease after an inquiry of the subject area. Tom agreed to the idea. "Anything you can do to stop this mess would be a blessing!" he exclaimed. I was careful to make no promises.

Meditation of a 'clearing' nature must be conducted with a tremendous degree of protection. Permission to go forward with this work was granted by a loud "Yes!" during prayer the morning following my visit with Tom.

In this visualization I was shown Tom sitting in his living room watching television. His two dogs lay by his chair. I requested permission to go upstairs and visit the children. Quickly, they came into my vision 'out of curiosity and boredom.' Amy appeared to be nine or ten years of age, garbed in a Victorian dress. She held hands with a young girl slightly older and taller. No name was offered for her. Both girls had lived during the 1860s period in America. A third child— a small boy —sullen and shy stood slightly apart from the girls. He acted reluctant to participate.

Amy and her companion said that 'this looked like a great adventure to them and like lots of fun.' Eva Turner, while living on the earth plane, enjoyed accumulating a haven for spirits. She had promised each child safety forever, in addition to plenty of people and pets to play with. But the children were tired of the game. No one who'd lived in the house liked them. The animals were always frightened of them.

During the meditation I showed them the direction toward the bright light, as well as the *Twenty-seven Steps* toward the Light. Amy had always wanted a kitten. Now at the far end of the Light, she saw her kitten. The two girls moved upward happily. The boy was pouting; he hated to be left behind. Suddenly a lithe young woman dressed in a beige outfit, of the 1860s period, manifested beside the boy. The woman had the presence of a governess.

While the boy took her outstretched hand, the pair stepped into the Light simultaneously. The governess made an unusual comment, "We must go quickly so that the 'others downstairs' won't miss us right away." She glanced over her shoulder to see if they were being watched.

Two weeks later I returned to visit Tom. My mother Carolyn Morrison accompanied me as we stood near the front porch. This trip I experienced none of the oppressive energy as during my first visit. However, what remained seemed to be directed toward Carolyn. A headache, difficulty in breathing and heavy lethargy overtook her in minutes.

Tom was feeling lighter, somewhat relaxed. His first comment was that all of the unusual activity had ceased the day after my previous visit. Nothing out of the ordinary had occurred during the past two weeks. Only 'after' his comments did I mention to him anything of the 'clearing' meditation.

"I have no understanding of what you are doing, but I'm certainly grateful to you," Tom declared. After the brief meeting, we departed and arranged for me to stop again before he moved out of the vicinity.

This I did late in December. Tom was pleased to report that none of the formidable activities had reoccurred. Although some of the energies remained, the worst had ceased. The undeniable cold remained throughout the house. Tom's temper frequently raged at the new roommate who'd recently arrived. This rage was not 'logically' accounted for and unfamiliar to Tom.

As we departed my father, Glen Morrison, who accompanied me this last visit left with a nasty headache— one of only four he'd ever had in seventy-five years. Possibly the laughing children are gone. Yet one thing is certain— much of the House of Spirits remains intact.

[The life story of Eva, her practices, works regarding Tchaikovsky, are well-documented at the University of Virginia. In recent years one graduate student's thesis in parapsychology was written entirely on her life previous to her death in 1994.]

The Wilderness

Yankee cannon tore the woods apart. Grape, canister, shell exploded like a tornado out of a clear sky and burst upon the forest. Fallen tree limbs, branches and whole trees fell upon the Rebels. Bark from the trees stung their faces while splintering wood from saplings stuck in their clothes. Union officers watched Rebs charge in solid waves, three deep. 5th and 6th Alabama, Colonel Daniel Christie's 23rd North Carolina, Dole's 44th Georgia, 30th North Carolina, 10th Louisiana, and 4th North Carolina were among them.

As the battle in the Wilderness drew to a close, the losses were terrible. Ramseur's Brigade lost 623 out of 1,400 men. The 2nd North Carolina lost 214 soldiers from 340. The list of casualties stretched on. All around were scores of dead, both Union and Confederate. Artillery drivers raced to the front lines, their carriage wheels and horses' hoofs crushed and mutilated the bodies of friend and foe. Wounded soldiers by the hundreds lay by the Plank Road, their bodies sheltered from the sun by blankets held up by muskets stuck in the ground from the bayonet upward.

Today Tom and Barbara Quigley live in Spottsylvania County in the midst of this battlefield. Bayonet's, spoons, and other Civil War relics have been unearthed in their backyard. Less than three miles away, Stonewall Jackson was mortally wounded by one of his own men. Yet, the visitations inside their home are easily as dramatic as the history on its outside.

One morning in 1994 Mrs. Quigley entered the room of her older daughter. "Wake up. You have to drive your sister to school," Barbara said.

"Yeah, get up!" repeated a male voice coming from within the room. She turned around, knowing that her husband had already left for work. No one was in sight. Yet, the young male voice began to sing a lullaby.

That was enough for Barbara. She left the room and went toward the downstairs. Someone in vapor-like fashion followed her down the steps. As she entered the kitchen, the radio on the counter stopped working.

The following Monday at 11:30 a.m. Barbara was scrubbing the kitchen floor. "Can I help you?" offered a male voice. She spun around to greet her husband. Again there appeared to be no one around.

6:00 p.m. of that day Kristen, the younger daughter, was up in her room talking on the phone with a girlfriend. Suddenly her parents heard her screaming as though she'd been hurt. The two ran upstairs to her rescue. "What is wrong with you?" they asked.

While talking on the phone, Kristen had been interrupted by a man's voice from behind her. "What are you doing?" he wanted to know. But as Kristen looked up, she found no visible source for the voice.

A month passed with no activity from their spirit. It resumed one morning when Barbara rose early from sleep. Returning from downstairs, she felt a presence follow her up the steps. She entered the bedroom and closed the door behind her. Still she sensed another's presence. Barbara got back in bed beside her husband who remained sleeping. As she curled up next to Tom, the weight of a third person sat on the bed beside her. She felt the mattress depress while the invisible form moved again. Barbara could only move closer toward Tom and wait for the spirit to depart.

This experience was not to be a singular event. Barbara recalls four other occasions of similar occurrences. "Each time if I speak loudly or scream, it disturbs the energy and it leaves," she explains. "I was somewhat envious of people who claimed to have seen or felt ghosts. Since none of these things had ever happened to me, I really didn't believe it possible," Barbara says. "But when I witnessed them personally in my own house, that's another story. Sometimes this guy whistles or sings an old-fashioned lullaby. I'm certain that he is a young man in his early twenties from the sound of his voice."

Most of the incidents seem to happen in Kristen's room or in the hallway. There are times when the cat will be sitting alone in the hallway. Suddenly it'll jump up and run to scratch on a door as if to get away from something. Frequently they will hear a noise in Kristen's room similar to the sound made by someone blowing air across the top of an empty bottle.

Early January, 1995 Kristen sensed someone descending the staircase. As she turned to look toward it, she assumed it was her mother. This flowing figure completely dressed in red, appeared as a woman. "Mom, is that you?" Kristen asked. The apparition vanished while Barbara answered from the opposite direction.

Tom Quigley tells of a neighbor's frightening experience only a short distance down the road. "She and a friend were riding their horses recently. All of a sudden, they were enveloped by the sounds of an entire herd of horses running toward them! They nearly panicked when they felt as though they'd be trampled. Still as they scanned the vicinity, no other animals could be seen," Tom explains.

Research on the area reveals interesting details. The Quigley home is in the midst of Pickett's encampment. While the horse-owner's property lies within a mile of the Quigleys' home, it was the area where the 4th U.S. Cavalry made its mass charge down that same road. Jackson ordered a flank attack on Union lines. This was the Union cavalry's response.

Haunting at the Mill

"That Cummins Jackson was quite a character," offered Dorotha. "He's well-known for having raised his nephew 'Stonewall' Jackson as a child. But around here in Weston and the Jackson's Mill area, he was a notorious individual," she said. "Folks living back then were pretty certain he had something to do with the haunting of the gristmill."

Dorotha Ramsburg Gaston lives in Weston, West Virginia near Jackson's Mill. She approached me during the spring of 1995 with unrecorded information regarding the historic mill, as well as Cummins Jackson.

She was fourteen years old the first year she attended 4-H Camp at Jackson's Mill in 1924. Until that time Dorotha had never heard about the haunting of the mill. Disbelieving the mysterious tale, she went home to learn what her father knew of it.

Arvil Ramsburg assured her it was true. "Yes, it was haunted at one time. We heard the sounds while we lived there." He reminded his daughter that he, his sister and parents had lived in the same log cabin in which Stonewall was raised. Arvil continued, "My daddy was running the mill at the time. Our family had operated it since 1850 when your great-grandfather John Wesley Ramsburg was there. Several of us heard that mill running on its own late at night, long after its doors were locked. Now if you don't believe me, go ask your Aunt Gay. She was in on it too."

Dorotha knew her aunt to be a truthful, serious lady. Everything was black and white, no in-betweens. The young girl marched over to her aunt's house. She was determined to hear as much as possible about Jackson's Mill.

"Oh yes, I lived there and I heard the noises!" Aunt Gay said emphatically. "Many nights long after the mill was shut down and the workers had locked up and were long gone, we could hear it start up again. We were responsible for taking care of it, so one of us had to walk down over the knoll. Often times it was me that did that," her aunt recalled. "I'd get the keys to the doors, then strike out in the dark to see who was down there. As soon as I put the key in the lock, those sounds would stop."

"What were the sounds like?" Dorotha wanted details.

"It sounded exactly like the gristmill was working. There's no mistaking what the noise was," her aunt replied. "A few times I got as near as the paling fence before the mill quit. As I pushed open the gate, those noises quit."

Dorotha asked, "What caused it?"

"We never knew for certain, but we were pretty sure we found out the source. The drummers came through our area frequently. They'd stop at all the homes to peddle their wares, but ours was the last house on the dirt road. That meant that they usually stayed overnight with us," Dorotha's aunt remembered it well. "Several of the drummers heard the noises too. They were pretty scared of it. One fella stopped coming to our house because he was so frightened.

"One day a drummer who badly needed shoes for his horse stopped at the mill. The horseshoe pit used to be right between the paling fence and the mill," Aunt Gay went on. "There was no iron to be used for those shoes. We searched the property for scrap iron. Finally, someone suggested that they look up in the attic of the mill. Nobody ever went up there anymore, but it had been used for storage long ago," explained her aunt.

"One of the men went through the attic. When he returned, he was carrying an iron rod about two feet long, with dark red stains all over it," the woman described the scene. "Those stains were a real puzzle. They weren't rust and didn't seem like paint. Furthermore, none of us had ever seen that rod around the mill before.

"The men melted down the rod to make those horseshoes. From that day on, those mysterious sounds from the mill ceased," Aunt Gay said. "We began to put two and two together. The story of Cummins murdering a man by hitting him with a blunt object had previously been circulating through the community. So then these folks figured that this piece of iron was the murder weapon. And, they were also convinced that the iron rod's connection to the murder was the cause of the mill working on it's own at night."

The young girl listened intently. She realized that she was learning pieces of history that weren't found in her school books. "Whatever happened to Cummins?" she asked.

Her aunt replied, "He used to hang around the mill a lot when our folks ran it. His good buddy, Jesse James, the outlaw, hung around with him, too. Daddy used to feel so sorry for that big ole mule Jesse rode. It was the most swaybacked animal he'd ever seen. Jesse's feet would drag the ground when he rode the mule.

"Yep, Cummins Jackson and Jesse James were pretty 'thick,'" her aunt mused. "Cummins was doin' a considerable amount of counterfeiting of silver coin, too. The Feds knew it, but they just hadn't been able to find the location where he was working. They warned him repeatedly," she said. "Finally Cummins left the area because of it. Ole Jesse disappeared with him. Jesse was originally from Clay County, Missouri. So the two of 'em headed back out West."

Dorotha was intrigued by it all. She resolved to talk with her father more about the story. Once at home Dorotha quizzed him further about his experiences.

He readily complied. "The Ramsburgs left Jackson's Mill for a bit to run the mill at Weston. During the Civil War, Union troops would come in and steal our lumber. We were leaning more toward the Confederate sympathies," Arvil explained. "At one point your great-grandfather was so afraid he'd be taken prisoner that he jumped into the river and swam toward the state hospital. Not long after that icy swim, John developed pneumonia and died."

Her father remembered more, "After the war we returned to Jackson's Mill for a short while. I was fishing beside the bridge near the mill one afternoon. My line got stuck among some tree roots where I was sitting. It was the strangest thing about that line," he commented. "Down among those root's was lodged a rusty tin box. I dug it out of the dirt and roots. I could tell it'd been well-sealed. When I opened it, piles of disintegrated paper fell out. We were certain that it was part of Cummins' stash of money." Arvil grinned while recalling his discovery. "I was determined to find more of it, too. Benny, who lived in town. finally admitted to me that he'd helped Cummins with his counterfeiting. But he swore to his death that he'd never tell where or how they worked."

A Shallow Grave

October 9, 1993 Agnes and Thomas Haldane arrived at the new home of their daughter and son-in-law in Findley, Ohio. The house is situated in a new development known as Western Meadows. Here they planned to stay a short period of time while looking for a home of their own.

2:30 a.m. of her first night in this home, Agnes was awakened from a sound sleep. She walked to the bedroom door and opened it. In front of her stood a man six feet tall, dressed in a blue uniform coat mid-thigh in length with eight brass buttons. His trousers were a darker shade of blue. The solider appeared to be quite ill as his cheeks were sunken and his cheekbones protruded noticeably. He leaned against the door frame in order to stand upright. His black hair was cut close and parted on the left side.

Agnes distinctly received the information that he was ill with pneumonia or tuberculosis. As soon as she made out these details, he faded away from her vision.

Both Agnes and Thomas are comfortable working with the spiritual realms. However, the two lacked knowledge regarding the Civil War in the Findley area. A visit to the county library that following day would clear that up.

They learned that while there was no combat in that immediate area, there had been Union encampments. Some of the military personnel had even brought their families with them. Midst their reading about the war, they discovered an exact description of an officer's uniform comparable to that of Agnes' apparition.

Since this experience of October 9, Agnes has learned more from older residents. Many of the Union soldiers, who died of wounds or illness elsewhere, were often brought to Findley for burial. Frequently these graves were shallow.

Agnes and Thomas are certain that the digging for the foundations of these new homes has disturbed the spirits lying below.

Fort Clinch

A reenactor with a New York infantry regiment and veteran policeman of several years, Jim realized how startled he was as he lay in bed listening to his uninvited company. "I distinctly heard what sounded like heavy benches being scooted around on the wooden floor," Jim recalls. "It was accompanied by the sounds of heavy breathing and sobbing, as though someone were crying."

The scene was Fort Clinch, a state park in Fernandina Beach, Florida. Jim's reenactment group had chosen to bunk in the enlisted men's barracks. However distinct the sounds had been, two boys slept soundly nearby. Yet, Jim was certain of what he'd experienced in the dark confines of the fort.

He mentioned the occurrence to a female staff member at the park the next day. She assured him that he wasn't 'crazy' as some of his buddies were trying to convince him. Many people had reported incidents substantiating the 'haunting' theory. Among these were various park rangers who'd observed Civil War soldiers walking across the drill field on moonlit nights. The only parts of their bodies visible were the top halves, never their legs.

Saturday night Jim had a similar experience. He was fast asleep when he was awakened by the same sounds as the previous night. "The visitor moved to the opening between the NCO room and the enlisted room. It remained there for quite a while," Jim vividly remembers the circumstances. "The fire in the fireplace had gone out, so the rooms were black as pitch. But from the sounds, I knew it was so close to me that I could have pointed with a finger and with certainly say, 'it's right here!' If it had been a matter of me and an armed criminal, I would have known exactly where to point my weapon. It was so close I could have about reached out and touched it," Jim says. "It was apparent that it didn't intend to harm anyone. Maybe it was curious about why we were there.

Robert packed up his gear. He'd seen enough— time to get out of this place! Living History or not, in all of his years reenacting with the 15ᵗʰ New York Corps of Engineers, Robert had never seen anything so 'weird.'

His friend Bob saw him leave his guard post and head for his gear. Bob went over to check on him, "Hey, man, what's up? What're you doing?"

"I was up on my post at the front gate. When I looked back across the parade field, there was a Union soldier walking toward me," Robert described the situation. "I assumed it was another reenactor. The guy continued walking straight at me! Eventually he got close enough that I saw he was wading through the ground; it only came up to his knees!" Robert was genuinely disturbed by the experience. "When this 'thing' walked past me, it had no face, just a soldier's body from the knees up! The icy chills ran all over me. I had to get out of there."

As soon as the opportunity arose, Bob approached one of the rangers. He recounted the incident. The ranger's response was quite matter-of-fact. "Oh yeah, several people have reported the same sightings," he said. The ranger explained part of the mystery on observing only parts of the bodies. "The original Civil War period level of the parade field was one-and-a-half to two feet lower than present conditions. Because Fort Clinch is close to the sea, storms and other weather conditions have filled in dirt and sand as time has passed," he said.

Have You Stood at Cold Harbor

by
James H. Taylor

Come on a day when you come alone—For they were alone—
    yet together
Each alone when life went so quickly, or together if
    so slowly in pain.
So stand there and thank God for your own.

Look at this place how quiet, how peaceful, and remember
    the day it was not—When life's promise went
    unfulfilled for so many, unanswered for each.

If you bow your head down and do them their honor, they
    may answer in waves of anguish unheard. If they
    do you will know it in a presence that will linger
    in your heart as it lingers in mine.

So go stand at Cold Harbor but stand there alone.

Tour by Candlelight

Are the phantom spirits at Kenmore Mansion lingering from the Revolutionary War period? Or did some remain behind when it was a field hospital during the Battle of the Wilderness? On the evening of December 4, 1994 thirty-five individuals witnessed the anger of an invisible force.

Kenmore Mansion is the beautiful home built by Colonel Fielding Lewis. The artistry and design of two centuries are combined to demonstrate many examples of our nation's heritage. To personify Kenmore's involvement in America's Civil War, each December the 1st and 44th Georgia Infantry Regiment reenactors stage scenes as the Fredericksburg house was used for medical care after the fighting.

Approximately 7:45 p.m. on December 4, the Living History program became livelier than expected. The tour groups had been nonstop all day. The public's curiosity regarding hospital scenes and leg amputations brought a heavy response. The five reenactors were reliving a particularly graphic scene involving a Confederate surgeon, assistant surgeon, and a member of the Ladies' Aid Society working on a patient. This scene was arranged in Kenmore's dining room where the original surgery was performed.

Darkness had fully penetrated the room. A second set of beeswax candles was retrieved from a haversack. A few oil lamps lit the rooms, with a candle lantern and a candle in a holder placed on a field desk to aid in illumination of the surgery area. As Mark narrated the portrayal for their last audience, all eyes were riveted on the amputation scene. The candle separated from its holder, levitated two and a half feet straight up in mid-air, and flew five feet across the room to impact the base of the wall. It was such an unusual movement with such force that everyone stood in awe in a hushed silence.

As soon as Mark was able to move, he rushed over to the candle lying on a mattress tick full of straw. Nothing had caught on fire. Still, no one spoke. Everyone filed outside quietly.

The reenactors began packing up their gear. Someone turned on the electric floor lights. Mark was still curious about the candle incident. He got down on his hands and knees, examining the floor where the object landed with such a dramatic impact. There was absolutely no wax spilled or broken in the area. Only a slight smudge spot remained on the wall as proof of what had happened. "We weren't scared at all," Mark commented on behalf of the people in his unit. "But we had the impression that whoever was there only wanted to get our attention and recognition of its presence."

The candle at Kenmore Mansion.

John Gosselin

91

Fort McAllister

The woman advanced menacingly toward Kurt. She had her two bawling kids in tow. Kurt, a reenactor from the 44th Georgia Infantry, calmly maintained his post. His unit was on hand conducting candlelight tours of Fort McAllister, part of the Savannah defenses.

"Look, I know it's Halloween, but you guys have really gone too far with this!" the woman screamed in his face. "My kids are terrified!"

Kurt responded innocently, "What is the problem, Madame?"

"That headless soldier over there is too gory! All you can see is blood dripping over his shoulders and chest!" The woman was pointing toward a battery once commanded by Major Gilmore during the war. The angry mother continued her graphic description of the headless man's uniform, as well as how wildly he'd flailed about with his sword.

Kurt assured her that no reenactors were portraying a headless soldier.

Completely unaware of the scene during that day of Fort McAllister bombardment, the frantic woman and her children had witnessed the suspension of energy through 'time.' At that battery post so many years ago, Major Gilmore had stuck his head out over the parapet during one of the sieges. He was instantly decapitated by enemy fire. His body had walked on a few feet before toppling over. Even then it fell on his sword handle which propped the body up momentarily.

Whether Gilmore was killed by shelling from the "Montauk" or one of the other monitors isn't certain as the Federals pounded the earthworks of McAllister unsuccessfully many times. Major Gilmore and the garrison's favorite cat were the only two casualties at Fort McAllister during the Civil War.

Another Time, Another Place

Pauline and her four year old daughter Kelley were recently transplanted to Richmond, Virginia from Massachusetts. Today Pauline was driving them on a Sunday tour of the Richmond area. Hollywood Cemetery, final resting place for numerous Civil War soldiers, was coming up on their right.

"Mommy, look!" Kelley was pointing wistfully out of the car window. "I was killed in that war. My body is buried over there."

For many years Jon Phillips has had serious feelings towards past lives. Recently he took the opportunity to explore Regression Hypnosis. During his first session with a hypnotist, he experienced himself as a teenage boy in an eastern American mountainous area, possibly Pennsylvania. He was kidnapped by a Native American raiding party and taken a long distance to their village.

Jon recalls the visual images in this session as extraordinary. Hiding from the raiders in a well, he vividly recognized his two captors peering down at him, then hauling him out. The Indian on the left wore an elaborate mantle of white feathers about his shoulders. The following scene was of the burning buildings in the valley below as Jon's guards escaped with him captive and tied. Eventually, they arrived at a village beside a stream whose bottom was covered with mossy rocks. He was raised to young adulthood, and much later was forced to return to white civilization, quite unhappily.

Continuing with this session, Jon experienced himself further along in adulthood. He stood in front of a stone house, holding a rake in his hand. Reluctantly, he was telling the hypnotist that he was a tenant whose name was Ben. "How nosy she is to ask!" Ben had thought.

Jon was even more curious about regression than previously. He learned more about relaxation techniques. He began reading further on the subject and continued practicing the techniques on his own.

One of his most cherished scenarios took place on the western slope of Little Roundtop at Gettysburg. Near the bottom of that slope and in line with where the 44th New York Monument now stands, Jon finished his life as a soldier of the Civil War. His body lay in a prone position wedged between two large rocks. His head was toward the north. Through the pitch darkness, two men with a lantern approached him from above. The men directed the light down on him and declared their sorrow at his mournful condition. They moved on and complete darkness descended.

Hundreds of people today strongly sense that they participated in America's Civil War. These individuals differ remarkably in their backgrounds, knowledge of history, occupations, and their ages. More people than ever before are exploring avenues seeking whatever lay in their past.

Dent Meyers of Kennesaw, Georgia is among those curious people. So many 'coincidences' in his life strongly indicate that he lived as Stonewall Jackson. Just as Jackson suffered a severe wound to his left arm, resulting in amputation, which led to pneumonia and his death, Dent Meyers also suffers from similar pain running up his left arm. That pain originates from the exact area of the arm where Jackson was hit. Stonewall was born on January 21st, whereas Mr. Meyers' birth date is January 29th. The physical resemblance between the two men is astounding. Dent's facial characteristics are so similar to Jackson's that he has played the role of the general in several movies, such as "Stonewall Jackson's Way." He has also sat for several artists' portraits. William Maughn's painting "The Prayer

Warrior" and Hong Min Zou's "Tribute to the Cause" are two fine examples.

Now retired, Dent began his reenacting career in 1961 when he joined the 1st Georgia Volunteers as a private. He later transferred to the 44th Georgia Infantry and on to the 1st Georgia Light Artillery Division. He eventually commanded the entire Georgia Division for nine years prior to concluding his active participation in 1991.

None of this information was available to Doc Anderson, a psychic reader from Rossville, Georgia. Several years ago Dent requested a reading from the well-known psychic. The information offered quite strongly that Mr. Meyers had lived previously as Stonewall Jackson.

Even though he is 'officially' retired from Civil War reenacting, Dent remains active in that community. From his business, Wildman's Civil War Surplus at Kennesaw, he keeps the Southern Spirit alive through memorabilia and reminiscences.

One of his favorite experiences with Doc Anderson occurred during Doc's visit to Dent's home at Gilgale Church, a battlefield area. Anderson pitched a tent on the battlefield with the intention of contacting some of the soldiers. The evening began as a beautiful moonlit night. The assembled group proceeded with a trance session. Almost immediately a terrific cloudburst descended and doused the campfire. The downpour was intense, yet one soldier from many years ago came through to them. He remained long enough to offer numerous details to them. As soon as the trance session was complete, the weather cleared as mysteriously as it had advanced upon them.

Dent feels that this solider periodically now visits him in his home. "First a severe coldness will manifest," Dent describes the sensation. "I'll know he's going to stay a while. Several of my personal belongings will be spontaneously moved around. One of the rugs in my den especially is constantly being shoved aside," he continues. "Then upstairs, too, the rugs will be completely rolled up and moved. Other objects will be hidden from me, then reappear when I'm least expecting it."

Through the years Mr. Meyers has come across some unusual artifacts. A cap box from the Civil War was the most intriguing. A hunter living in Pauldin County had been using it to carry .22 caliber shells. This man had originally discovered the box in a very old house in the New Hope vicinity. The artifacts produced there had been untouched for many years. As soon as the man carried the cap box into his home, unusual and frightening manifestations began occurring there. The hunter was convinced that all this was directly associated with the box.

Dent became curious about the artifact, and the hunter was eager to part company with it. From the time he first took the cap box into his home, Dent found it difficult to sleep at night. The energy associated with it was dreadful.

He approached a group of psychics in Atlanta, asking them to perform psychometry readings on the cap box. One woman reached out to take it in her hands. Abruptly, she drew away from it in fear. A second reader in another room was, however, able to handle it.

The information he offered was clear. "This once belonged to a psychotic killer," the reader said. "I see a man in a gray uniform who truly enjoys killing other people." To Mr. Meyers this indicated a Confederate soldier who'd probably been a sniper. Nevertheless, it was Dent's turn to rid himself of the box.

Dent Meyers at Fort Pulaski during the filming of "Ordeal of Dr. Mudd"—September-November, 1979.

Courtesy of Dent Meyers

Meadow Farm

Luke Denton, one of the youngest members of the 3rd U.S. Regulars reenactment group, had an unusual experience with the female spirit at Meadow Farm. October, 1993 Luke was portraying one of the Sheppard children during the filming of a documentary. His 'sister' Susan sat with him in the upstairs classroom. The two of them played checkers near the window.

Susan, a blonde-haired, blue-eyed eight year old, looked out the window and returned a wave from two Meadow Farm employees. Luke moved closer to the window. He also waved down at the people standing in the front yard.

Sometime later that afternoon, one of the employees approached Luke. "Who was that at the window standing between you and Susan this morning?" she asked.

Luke was surprised at the question. "There wasn't anyone up there but me and Susan."

"Yes there was. I saw a woman taller than either of you. She had dark hair and wore a dark purplish colored dress of an 1860's period costume," the employee insisted. Afterwards they would realize that the female she described fit the description of Virginia Sheppard who lived there years ago before her 'death.'

Virginia Young Sheppard grew up at White Chimneys Plantation in Caroline County. She married Dr. John Sheppard in 1846. Together they raised ten children at their beautiful home in Henrico County. While John Sheppard maintained a successful medical practice, his cherished Meadow Farm became a thriving tobacco farm. This prosperity ended, however, with the advent of the Civil War.

As was customary during times of war, Virginia Sheppard probably stayed with her farm as Philip Sheridan's troops stormed through the area. By her steadfast attitude, she likely saved Meadow Farm from destruction.

The first mention that the Meadow Farm employees heard of the phantom was from a security related incident a few years ago. One of the security men answered an alarm there. He made an off-hand remark about the lady behind the curtain.

The employee's remarks were joking, "Oh yeah. Sure there is."

"I'm serious," he exclaimed. "Some evenings when I ride out here to check the grounds, there's frequently a lady upstairs, pulling back the curtains and looking out at me."

Nevertheless, the matter was not pursued further at the time.

However, the second sighting followed not long after that. A community service volunteer arrived ahead of schedule one Sunday morning. Since none of the staff was there to let him in, he and his nephew waited on the front porch. The young boy turned to his uncle and commented, "There's somebody here. I saw her in the window."

With this both of them turned toward the house. The woman was still at the window watching them. Convinced that someone was inside who could let them in, they knocked on the door.

Still, no one answered.

At 9:00 a.m. the staff worker arrived. The volunteer explained how they'd tried to go in, but the woman inside wouldn't open the door. The staff member unlocked the door, setting off the alarm. He knew fully that no one was inside. Otherwise the burglar alarm would have been turned off.

"But she was there! We both saw her looking straight down at us!" the youth and his uncle insisted. A thorough search inside the house proved that no one was present.

Nannette Morrison

David Hanna, Keith Holman, Daniel Hanna, Luke Denton, and Peter Holman at Meadow Farm—June, 1995. Luke reenacts with the 3rd U.S. Regulars. Others are with 83rd PA Vols.

Later in 1993 a young man from Virginia Commonwealth University visited Meadow Farm to work on his internship. It was 4:00 p.m., all the tours had been completed at 3:30 p.m. The student sat with staff workers discussing future programs at the farm.

Someone below began knocking on the front door. One woman departed in order to answer the door. As she reached the downstairs door, the intern's girlfriend greeted her, "I'm sorry to disturb you. I know you have a tour upstairs."

The woman responded, "No, we don't have a tour. We were just meeting in my office."

"Well, I looked up at the far right bedroom window and saw a lady looking out," the young woman explained.

Regardless of what she'd witnessed, the only people present were in the Staff Office.

Mary is another Meadow Farm volunteer. She enjoys presenting spinning demonstrations at the farm. When she learned of the previous story, Mary came forward with her own version of a sighting of Mrs. Sheppard. "I didn't say anything about this before because I didn't want anyone to think I was crazy," she began to tell what she saw. "One day as I went up to the Staff Office, I passed that same far bedroom. I glanced into the doorway, and there stood a woman in a beautiful dress, gazing out the window. Her dress was dark-colored with rather a small print to it, an 1860's period dress. It was so becoming to her that I thought to compliment her on it when I returned. A few minutes afterward as I approached that door again, I could barely see the skirt of the dress disappear into the next room." Mary sounded disappointed, "I never saw her again after that."

Olustee

Martin didn't believe in 'spooks,' or spirits either for that matter. If it wasn't solid, if he couldn't touch it, it didn't exist. Martin had been on the police force most of his adult life. He figured he'd already experienced most of the frightening possibilities. But then again—Martin had never been to Olustee Battlefield.

He accompanied two of his friends to the historical site late one night in July, 1995. Because the others were 'firm believers,' Martin went along only to humor them. The trio dispersed to various directions of the site. Martin soon found himself alone just inside the wood line.

Suddenly crashing through the woods, a creature of enormous size sounded as though it would trample him! And it was close, 'very' close indeed! Martin barely had time to move. From the sound of its advancing loud footfalls, he expected a horse or at least a bear to mow him over. Martin screamed; he was terrified.

Wallace was by his side instantly. He yelled, "Stop!" at the top of his lungs. At the same time he snapped on his flashlight. Then— nothing.

There was no animal, no person in sight to threaten them. Yet, both men were sure they were going to be trampled. That night, as well as the following morning, all three men searched the area for footprints or broken branches. There'd been a burn in the immediate area recently, but no prints lay in the ashes. The sandy soil of Olustee should have offered up heavy prints from the intruder. Still, no evidence could be found of any animal small or large.

Martin now 'believes.'

On February 7, 1864 Brigadier General Truman Seymour's 7,000-man division landed at Jacksonville, Florida and marched westward to engage the Confederates. On February 20th Seymour led 5,500 of his Federal troops in a poorly-planned assault against 4,600 Rebs near Olustee. The Confederates stood firm in the assault, then counterattacked. Led by Brigadier General Joseph Finegan, the Rebs charged the disorganized Union troops.

Among Seymour's force were three black regiments. One of these, the 8th Colored Troops, lost as many as 310 men. The fighting in all battles is fierce. But because of the presence of these fighting black Union men, there was added hatred and resentment. The Georgia boys were particularly incensed at being attacked by the Colored Troops. History records how unfortunate was their treatment of the fallen soldiers.

Richard and the men in his Union reenactment unit were gathered outside the museum at Olustee. Some of them were playing Civil War period music, lending an authentic camp atmosphere to the early evening. Richard separated from the group and headed behind the museum, toward the Confederate Monument in the field beyond. As the one building is white, it offered a stark contrast for what he saw next.

A dark shadow about the height of a man, was walking in the direction from which Richard had just come. The form was not a definitive silhouette of a man, but a cylinder of energy which passed around the side of the building. Richard walked around front and rejoined his unit. He asked of a friend, "Did anybody just go behind the building?"

"Nobody but you," was the reply.

"You're not going to believe this, but I just saw a ghost go around the corner there!" Richard exclaimed. Afterwards he described how several of the guys felt as though their bodies were 'lighting up' much of that night. "We'd feel that electrical tingling sensation where your skin prickles, especially along the back of your neck," is how he explained it.

A little further into the evening, another reenactor suggested that they walk around a bit. He led the way toward the Union Monument. There lies buried in a mass grave, bodies of the black, as well as the white, infantrymen who fell at Olustee. For years a wooden cross marked the spot of the grave. Shortly after the turn of the century, that cross disappeared. Union reenactors built the present-day monument in recent years.

The closer the men came to the monument, the more aware they became of the eerie atmosphere. There was a full moon out and the sky had begun to cloud over. The air was full of electricity. Samuel, whose grandfather was a Cherokee Indian shaman, was among the band of men. He stepped near the Union Monument. "Richard, I think they have the monument in the wrong place," he spoke in a tentative voice.

His friend approached the area in which he was standing. "I stepped directly into what I sensed as an energy field," Richard said. "I could step through its periphery and feel it pass by me as I moved in. Then I experienced the same as I stepped out of it."

Their actions and comments began drawing more participants. More men joined them, as they formed a big oval gathering in the field. The psychic sensitivity passed from other generations was truly enhanced now. Samuel spoke again, "I think the dead are buried here, not over there exactly where the monument is."

This comment seemed to activate the reenactors even further. Three of these men were seasoned law enforcement agents. Yet, their training did not include this type of detective work. None of them knew what to expect. Each man walked around slowly, testing out the darkness.

Richard stepped into one area of trees. He thought he saw something flutter among them. Again, he found himself midst another ring of energy. Just as quickly, he was able to step out again. He said of its circumference, "I could go to the side of it and in again so that I virtually mapped out a specific area of energy." He said to Samuel, "Come down here." Richard was careful to step away from the energy field so as not to influence Samuel's perspective.

Nevertheless, Samuel immediately walked into it and froze. He paused very briefly before backing out of the energy field. He exclaimed, "I can't stand it! I can't stand it!"

"What happened there!" Richard asked.

"In my mind's eye, I saw that there were wagons here carrying in the bodies of the black troops. The Confederates were throwing them in a pit right here." Samuel was shaken by his vision. "There was one black soldier who was on his knees begging them not to kill him. But they shot him at point blank range at the edge of the pit and shoved him the rest of the way in." Samuel moved further away from the location. His impressions were too vivid and disturbing.

Richard led the entourage to another area. He suddenly came upon one energy pocket that affected him. Then as Samuel moved into it as well, he described his impressions of it, "I could see artillery working there." He offered more details of the area, all of which would later be confirmed completely.

The trail of reenactors continued, either by participation or by watching and listening. The group looked more like a row of ducks as they followed Richard and Samuel in their two-hour tour. At one point Richard spotted an old barbed wire fence running along the side of the field. He felt drawn to investigate. As he did so, Richard again experienced a strong energy field.

Samuel followed suit. "Ow!" came his instant reaction. He grabbed his shoulder and spun around. "I feel as though I've been shot in the shoulder!"

Another man among them, more familiar with the Olustee Battle, produced a book describing the action in 1864. On the very spot where Samuel stood, a Union officer had been wounded in the shoulder. It was in the immediate vicinity where the 54th Massachusetts fought.

Oliver and his son Timmy have had a special kinship with Olustee's spirits for fifteen years. Each visit they make is unique in its own way. Both of them welcome the interaction with the energies lingering there. One early March morning of 1995 was particularly exciting.

"We were driving past the large monument when my son pointed at a huge bubble of energy hovering in front of it," Oliver said. "I parked the car, and we walked over to the edge of this heavy mist. It was amazing! The day was gorgeous, clear, not a cloud in the sky. Yet here in front of us only a few feet off the ground was this oval shaped bubble of energy," Oliver continued his description. "It was approximately fifteen yards by twenty-five yards in size. The sides were smooth like glass. But the top had bumps on it, similar to the heads of men in military formation.

"We walked all the way around it while it hovered perfectly between the two smaller monuments," Oliver said. "At one point I couldn't resist sliding my arm into the wall of the fog. Geeze, it was icy cold in there! But that wall was so thick you could hardly see through it. Then we watched it slowly begin to circle the large monument and fade away as its circle was complete."

Oliver has mentioned some of his experiences at Olustee to a few people. The 'non-believers' scoff and say it's his imagination. However, on Oliver's mantel over the fireplace, he keeps a very solid reminder that so many 'things' are possible.

"I was standing beside the fence line one afternoon a few years ago," Oliver continued with his Olustee experiences. "Suddenly, I felt as though I was being watched. I looked up to see a person dressed in Union uniform watching me from the road. At first I thought he was metal detecting. So, I spoke to him and took a few steps toward the guy. The soldier simply side-stepped into the wax myrtle bushes and vanished.

"Well," Oliver resumed, "it still didn't dawn on me exactly what had happened. There were no footprints in the sandy soil. But as I looked down, I found a thin, clear, glass pocket flask where he'd been standing midst the tire tracks," Oliver said. "I know that road is traveled frequently, there'd been no recent reenactments, nor had there been any recent digging in the area.

"That pint bottle is no reproduction either. It's definitely a Civil War period piece. These days I keep it on my mantel to remind me that many things are possible," Oliver concluded.

The Wall

Glen was trying to complete a sentence; still there was that annoying crackling interference on the intercom. "What did you say?" Kelley couldn't quite catch his entire remark.

"I said, 'there continues to be some sort of electrical snapping on my end of the connection!' Can you hear it?" Glen asked.

Kelley heard it alright. He started to remark on it. But his intentions were interrupted by a soft, distant-sounding female voice, "Glen, Glen, Glen..."

"Who was that?" Kelley demanded. "Who's in the room with you?" Because of tight security in their business, no one had the authority nor supposedly the capability to listen in on their direct line of communication.

"Believe me, there's nobody here. This line is secure, but I heard her too!" Glen had electricity needling through his veins.

Kelley reacted the same way, "I believe you partner. I think we have ourselves a very unusual situation here." Kelley felt the hair rise on the back of his neck. Strange as it felt, the female voice on the security intercom did not come as a total surprise. He was certain this was one of two females who'd been attempting to contact both men for several days—a voice from the 'dead.'

The activity had become noticeable two weeks previous. Glen was at his station facing Brown's Island. Certain sections in the cement wall in front of him had begun to take on a life of their own. As Glen studied it further, he identified the shape of a woman, then another form of a female holding a child, another person handling a torch, a black woman beside the torch, and a black man sitting.

Glen switched on the private intercom, knowing that he had a direct line to Kelley. "Hey, I want to tell you what I'm seeing down here on this wall," Glen fully described the images to his partner.

Kelley had noticed them too, but had not mentioned it to anyone. He listened intently from several floors up, inside the building as Glen continued with his impressions. "Kelley, this is incredible! I feel as though these images are of people killed in the explosion during the war." While Glen focused his eyes on the wall, the second female's face began to stand out stronger. He experienced a sensation of anxiety which he realized was not his own. He recognized it as energy of sudden trauma those workers emitted so long ago.

Kelley agreed. As he closed his eyes and focused mentally on Glen's excited words, Kelley could also get impressions of the blast March, 1863. He began to hear a name..."Mary...Cushing...she was a fairly attractive woman, about twenty-two years old," Kelley continued describing the scene to Glen, "I'm certain that I can picture the buildings back then. They were long and white with black roofs." The information was so clear that both men were determined to obtain as many details as possible.

All of Kelley's details were verifiable. That same evening he read historical records on Tredegar Ironworks for the first time. Mary Cushing had been one of the forty people killed on Brown's Island as the Confederate Armaments Laboratories exploded. Another black laborer, also named Mary, was working with a board trying to get a friction primer loose. These were defective cartridges which the women were working on. As the cartridges were disassembled, the powder was put in one area and the empty cartridges in another.

Mary Ryan struggled with the board. Instead of taking the problem outside, she banged the object against a table. One spark was all it took to ignite the gun powder nearby.

For weeks after their discovery, the two men witnessed several unexplainable occurrences involving the building they work in. Electrical interferences on the intercom became frequent. A number of electrical shutdowns occurred on their security system. Two-hour investigations each time would never reveal the source of the problem. Two loud 'booms' in the vicinity were heard by various co-workers at the times of the shutdowns. Yet, the source of these were never located either.

Well over a hundred yards long, the wall was built in 1975 of concrete fitted with wooden forms. Only this one section directly looking onto where the Brown's Island explosion took place, bears any marks resembling people. Each of the remaining sections are exceptionally plain looking.

Glen and Kelley have the distinct impression that someone involved in that explosion of 1863 is reaching out, asking for help, and possibly for forgiveness.

A North Carolina Civil War Soldier's Memoirs

From "The Reminiscences of Berry Benson"

"Who knows but it may be given to us, after this life, to meet again in the old quarters, to play chess and draughts, to get up soon to answer the morning roll call, to fall in at the tap of the drum for drill and dress parade, and again to hastily don our war gear while the monotonous patter of the long roll summons to battle? Who knows but again the old flags, ragged and torn, snapping in the wind, may face each other and flutter, pursuing and pursued, while the cries of victory fill a summer day? And after the battle, then the slain and wounded will arise and will meet together under the two flags, all sound and well, and there will be talking and laughter and cheers, and all will say: Did it not seem real? Was it not as in the old days?"

The Stonewall Brigade

The day was a sultry one in July, 1976. Don wasn't certain what or who was drawing him to the Manassas Battlefield. He wandered alone south of the museum, drifting toward the two artillery pieces. The area sloping toward the woods especially beckoned him. Don sat down and gazed into the woodline.

Complete with blue uniforms and bayonets fixed, a solid line of soldiers appeared midst the grimy dust and heat waves rolling up from the ground. "Is this in my mind's eye, or am I actually seeing this happening?!" Don questioned himself. Brief as it was, he heard the drums roll. He saw the details of their faces—most of them bearded, perspiration trailing through the dust on the men's faces.

"Left oblique! Right oblique!" Officers gave commands, then more jumbled words. The soldiers advanced. Canteens and cups rattled at their sides. Rifles with bayonets were so terribly vivid.

Instantly, they were gone—vanished!

Today, Don Shannon is a lieutenant colonel in the U.S. Army. He has a strong military background, including one year of duty in Vietnam. He reflects on the mysterious sequence of events leading to the discovery of his relative Valentine Ripley. "I was six years old in 1950 when my dad first took me to Manassas Battlefield. I'm not certain why we went, other than the fact that I was curious about the Civil War but didn't understand it," Don says. "There were approximately twelve Civil War veterans still living at the time. Their photographs had recently been reproduced in the newspapers." These had created an impression on the boy.

"By the time I was eight, I was more interested in the war," Don continues. "Our family then visited Gettysburg. I was quite impressed with that. I was so intrigued by it that I questioned each of my grandparents, all living in Mount Jackson, to see if we had any relatives who had fought in the war. Each of them seemed pretty vague. This avenue produced no positive results other than a trip to the old cemetery near Union Church on route 11, once the Valley turnpike." The boy was discouraged, having no evidence of relatives participating in the Great Conflict. Eventually, Don forgot about the idea.

The years passed until Don spontaneously visited Manassas in July, 1976. 'Something' was pulling him back to Manassas. The experience that summer was so dramatic that he returned the following year. Nothing spectacular happened that next visit.

More years passed until December, 1983 when Don became quite ill. The illness spread so thoroughly that he was required to rest at home for two weeks. As he began to recover, a large red book in his library caught his attention.

Don flipped through its pages. A photograph of Union Church at Mount Jackson was displayed on page 18. He read that the 33rd Virginia Regiment had been raised at Mt. Jackson. Don was more than intrigued. He learned about Captain George Allen's infantry and numerous officers. The name Valentine Ripley stood out among them. It seemed unusual for a man's name. But the Ripley name was even more noticeable to Don. It was his mother's maiden name.

"Was it possible that this book, *Four Valiant Years in the Lower Shenandoah Valley*, held the answers to many questions?" Don wondered. He'd purchased it in July, 1977, the year of his third visit to Manassas. Yet, he'd never read it.

"I called my aunt who kept our family's Bible," Don continues. "She found Valentine Ripley in it. He was my great, great-grandfather!" Don relates happily. According to further information Valentine Ripley eventually became a first lieutenant in the 33rd Virginia.

Ripley's unit, as well as the 4th, 5th, 2nd, and 27th Virginia composed what officially became known as the Stonewall Brigade at First Manassas. The 33rd Virginia had lain behind that gentle sloping hill while batteries were being fired over them. These men wore the blue militia uniforms, easily confused with the Federal blues.

Don vividly recalls that July day of 1976. Could it be that he was actually staring at his 'lost' relative from the past? Valentine Ripley would have most certainly been among them.

Droop Mountain

The gray horse braced itself back on its haunches. He'd been ridden hard but was being abruptly reined in. His front legs had 'dried' mud spattered up to the shoulders. The gray's head was up high, neck arched, nostrils flared. The eyes were intense, staring directly at Ron. Those eyes glowed bright yellow like a cat's in the pitch dark of night!

No leather trappings were evident. Instead of a 'rider,' there was a gray 'wall' above the phantom's back. Later Ron would learn that he'd wandered onto part of Horse Heaven Trail where others have reported seeing a gray horse with a Confederate rider.

This was Ron Nelson's first year as a reenactor, 1990. He and Joe Hoff, also with the 17th Virginia Cavalry, Co. F., the Night Hawk Rangers, had traveled to Droop Mountain, West Virginia for the reenactment of that battle November 6, 1863. Neither man truly believed in ghosts or spirits as they trekked through the rainy night in search of the toilets.

Ron's flashlight beam wavered around a stack of picnic tables. "Hey Joe, look at that!" he shouted. "I didn't know there were any horses on this side of the mountain."

Assuming his companion saw the same horse he had several minutes before, Joe replied, "Yes, I guess there's just that one." Nothing more was said about it until much later. In the car ride home two days later, the two men compared notes in detail. Joe Hoff's chestnut horse with a white blaze face was far more solid than Ron Nelson's specter from one hundred twenty-seven years ago.

There are those people who are 'curious about the spirits. Having not seen one, they aren't certain they exist. Yet, there's that element where they cannot resist testing the possibility. At the point of contact, they don't always like what they see.

Jane was reenacting Civil War history with the 44th Virginia in 1992. The unit was camped at Droop Mountain on Halloween weekend to replay the scene for that battle. "We had heard some of the stories about the area, but none of us expected to see anything," Jane reports. Nevertheless, five members of their regiment walked along the Cranberry Bog Trail.

"We sat on a log for a short while and quietly discussed the event," Jane says. "Three of us saw a soldier appear, walking on the trail toward us. At first we thought it was another reenactor," she recalls. "But the closer it got, the eerier the situation became, We experienced the most uncomfortable sensations. Before us was a man in a blue uniform, a greatcoat, a hat, but with no facial features! He was definitely not a solid person.

"We'd had enough!" Jane exclaims. "We left in a big hurry! What was also strange was that three of us clearly saw him and the other two did not."

Sam stood atop the Lookout Tower playing 'Taps' for the 36th Virginia. This October evening 1992, darkness was descending quickly. Having completed the melancholy song, the bugler started down the tower steps. He had no desire to linger near dark at Droop Mountain.

He froze mid-way down the steps. Sam was stunned; his body wouldn't move. A few men from his company watched his curious actions from below. They called up to him. But Sam didn't respond.

He was seeing the Yankee army below the hillside. They'd spotted him in the tower and were pointing upward toward him. Sam was genuinely frightened. The experience was not of Yankee reenactors, but a sighting of Averell's men as they came from Hillsboro in 1863.

Two of Sam's buddies moved closer to him. "Come on down now. It's time we get back to camp." They were able to gradually ease him out of the situation. As Sam slowly accompanied them back to camp, the effects of the experience remained with him. Sam still felt as though he were moving in a daze.

Unfamiliar with the Droop Mountain roads, the Union reenactors had nearly lost their way back to camp. The night was getting late, while the heavy tree line cast thick shadows against few stars and sparse moonlight. They drove further into the battlefield area. As they arrived in a clearing, a Union sentry appeared in the road ahead.

Grateful for someone to give them directions, the men stopped their vehicle. "Howdy. Which direction is camp?" they inquired.

The soldier turned his ruddy face toward them. His response was vague, somewhat distant. He murmured an unintelligible remark about how close they were to town. His dirty and worn uniform seemed noticeably authentic.

The man driving the truck grew irritated. This man was a posted sentry but still was unable to give simple directions! The driver moved on a short distance and suddenly came upon the painted line marks for the park road. Only a few yards beyond the sentry, the driver executed a three-point turn in the road. He would give that 'idiot' a lesson in directions!

The instant he turned his truck, the sentry vanished. All of this having occurred in the open, there was no place for him to go. Shortly thereafter, they learned that no reenactor sentries had been posted in that vicinity.

It was 2:30 a.m. when Mr. Keen entered the curve on route 219 at the south side of the foot of Droop Mountain. He'd been driving the two-ton lumber truck since 3:30 a.m. the previous day. Tired, yet still alert, he was glad to be near home this morning in 1941.

Suddenly, Mr. Keen slammed on the brakes. Directly in the head-lights of his truck were eight to ten people riding on horseback, parade or fairground style. The men appeared to be dressed in military attire with khaki-colored pants, blue jackets and caps similar to those a chauffeur or army officer would wear.

The lead horse on the left side was white while the others were bay and darker colors. Mr. Keen distinctly saw saddle bags, typical of cavalry, on each horse. As the headlights caught them full on, the group veered sharply left and disappeared. Mr. Keen was out of his truck in a hurry to speak with them. Nowhere was there to be sight nor sound of the horsemen.

Marvin Keener was born in Nicholas County not far from Droop Mountain. Marvin's mother is Cherokee, one of the three tribes of Native Americans who inhabited the area long before the white man arrived. Some remained in the vicinity as the Civil War erupted.

On many a foggy night, according to members of Marvin's family who've witnessed this, the same Indian Chief who watched the battle at Droop Mountain can still be seen on the hillside. He stands majestically in full headdress beside route 219 in the area where the store is situated.

Mike Smith, Superintendent of Droop Mountain Park, has lived in it with his family for several years. He's had no personal experiences with the spirits lingering nearby. Although he considers himself to be a 'skeptic,' Mike does not entirely rule out all the stories surrounding Droop Mountain.

As one begins touring this beautiful, spacious battlefield park, you can leave your car near the park office. This is situated beside the superintendent's home where the Holbrook's story unravels. Years ago Mrs. Holbrook sat on the front porch and could hear footsteps approaching her from the rear. She rose from her seat to greet whomever was walking toward her. She saw no one. Instead, the footsteps proceeded toward the cellar house. At this point Mrs. Holbrook swore that she saw and heard the lock on the cellar house door move. Still the visitor was invisible.

In this same vicinity, there have been numerous reports from people hearing horses trot by, human screams of agony, and sightings of a Confederate soldier reclining against a tree.

During the Civilian Conservation Corps' development of the park in 1935, they had a small sawmill located where the parking lot is now. As that space was cleared, the bodies of about fifty soldiers were uncovered. These were relocated by the C.C.C. to an unidentified area. The Droop Mountain property was purchased for a park in 1928. It is the oldest state park in West Virginia. In the 1930's the C.C.C. began construction on various buildings there. In 1917-1918 when virgin timber was being cut from the mountain, one batch especially revealed much information on the paths of the bullets. The workers could follow a track of a bullet as it hit the trees and eventually could find its final resting place. Some days they were able to retrieve a gallon bucket of bullets.

As recently as 1940 people found horses' bones and teeth on the Horse Heaven Trail. This is the area where horses killed in the battle were disposed of. Today, one can look over Horse Heaven Rock and imagine how the carcasses might have been rolled over the edge.

Through these woods the buffalo and Indians trod the same route as visitors today or Civil War soldiers years ago. Route 219 had its beginning during those times. One can feel the life of the Senecas, Shawnees, and Cherokees as they inhabited Droop Mountain and surrounding counties.

If the athletic visitor is inclined to tour the park in winter, some of the trails offer wonderful cross-country skiing. The Cranberry Bog Trail is one of these. This was possibly the resting place of a Confederate cannon. Stories differ on this, however.

A gentleman from Virginia who traveled to Droop Mountain in recent years said that his grandfather had been a teamster with a Confederate artillery unit fighting at Droop Mountain. According to him, his grandfather had returned alone two or three weeks after the battle and hauled the cannon out of the Cranberry Bog. He claims to have taken it home, refitted it on a new carriage, and returned it to service.

Mike Smith seems to think, however, that the Union Army confiscated the cannon. In the official records of the 28th Ohio, among their List of Captured Material, is one twelve pound bronze howitzer. In these same reports is a statement of the capture of this cannon.

Another experience that is told about the area is that of the Snedegar sisters who roamed the battle site in the late 1880's while picking berries. The two women found two rifles from the 1863 engagement. The versions differ somewhat, but some accounts say that a high wind rose, trees and leaves thrashed wildly about so that the women were badly injured on their way home.

As they carried the guns inside their house, rocks flew through the walls and windows. An uncle came over to visit and was injured and frightened so badly that he soon departed. The fire in the fireplace acted strangely, the andirons jumped into the middle of the room dancing around, and a sheepskin rug rose into the air flapping around.

All this was too much for the Snedegar sisters. They moved the rifles to the barn, whereby a similar rock scenario ensued. Finally, the next day, the rifles were returned to Droop Mountain. All the unusual activity ceased.

On the walking tour of the battlefield, one can still cross the cattle guard where a Confederate foot soldier lost his life. During the fighting two Union cavalrymen who were brothers were chasing down the Reb. The younger brother always trying to outdo the older one, rushed forward, drew his saber, and chopped off the Reb's head. The head was slung into a nearby pond never to be found.

For many years afterward as horses were driven through this area, they would refuse to move on. The situation continued until the day a caravan of wagons passed through. The lead horses balked at moving forward. The driver proceeded to the front of the horses who were acting quite strangely. As the driver stood up on the traces between the animals, he identified the problem. The form of a man in a Confederate gray uniform stood holding the horses by their harness!

The driver beat the phantom about its shoulders until it turned the horses loose. The entity fell backward making horrible moaning sounds. Then it ran off into the woods. That was the last report of any difficulty regarding horses at that spot.

A related incident occurred in 1927 as Edgar Walton, accompanied by a friend, was walking home on a chilly evening. The two men tarried at Droop Mountain long enough to build a fire for warming themselves. Simultaneously, they looked at each other, both men suddenly experiencing extreme cold and a very creepy feeling. There was a soldier wearing a gray coat hovering above the ground nearby. It watched them a minute or so, then floated away into the trees.

Major Robert Augustus Bailey was the highest ranking Confederate killed in the battle of Droop Mountain. As the Confederates fell back, there was mass confusion. Cavalry rushed back through the infantry; all the units were mixed up. The Union Army was in sight of the highway, firing crossways into the horses. Wagons blocked the road, as well as artillery. Five thousand people were crammed into a one hundred fifty yard space. Bailey, commanding the 22nd Virginia Infantry, rallied fifteen to twenty men around him and attempted a rear-guard action. Their color bearer was shot, so Bailey retrieved the flag and was soon shot. The Old Soldier Trail was the site of this action during the battle.

The Musket Trail is named for the weapon found in a creek on Droop Mountain. The gun rests on display in the museum there. As recently as 1986, three boys discovered the Confederate Sharps carbine in the crags. The gun had once belonged to a soldier probably trying to escape down the side of the mountain. Midst the rocks and deep ravine, it's likely he became trapped. Shortly after the carbine's discovery, a gold wedding ring was located only eighteen inches from the exact spot.

The battle on the rugged mountain top was a miserably cold one that November. It snowed eight inches just two days after the fighting was over. Many of the soldiers would still have been out in those woods alone, possibly wounded and exposed to the elements.

The recorded deaths at Droop Mountain are two hundred seventy-five Confederates and one hundred nineteen for the Union. However, considerably more bodies have been discovered than are noted in the official records. The corpses were laid in shallow trenches with dirt over them. Within three weeks, wild hogs had discovered most of the bodies. The people of Hillsboro disinterred some of the remains, relocating them to Hillsboro, a few to a small cemetery on Droop Mountain, some to the Confederate Cemetery at Lewisburg. Another group relocated a few of the Union soldiers to the National Cemetery in Grafton. So much animosity remained after the war that most people did not wish to bury Confederate and Union men in the same cemetery.

This is considered to be the largest Civil War battle fought in West Virginia. Its importance lies largely in that it resulted in Confederate forces being driven into Virginia and fighting elsewhere. The Confederates never reoccupied the lost territory. Droop Mountain represented civil war in its truest and most tragic form. Brothers and neighbors fought under opposing flags. Former neighbors in the 10th West Virginia and the 19th Virginia met in very close combat on the left flank. One brother with the 22nd Virginia defended the right flank as the other brother fought against him defending their left flank.

The Devil's Armchair

From the beginnings of its recognition, Devil's Armchair was given its name by the Shawnee Indians. They were certain that it was haunted. Sitting prominently at the head of the valley, this out-cropping of rocks strongly resembled a huge chair with arms.

One night long ago a terrible storm came up. Lightning, high winds, and pounding rain tore through Montgomery White Sulphur Springs. The ensuing flash flood toppled over the Devil's Armchair, smashing it to pieces.

Prior to the Civil War, the valley located outside of Blacksburg was a health spa catering to the elite of society. Cabins lined the meadow, and the railroad conveniently laid a spur line into the re-sort. Very quickly, the resort became a booming, popular spot.

The advent of the war made it necessary for the health spa to be pressed into service as a hospital for Confederate soldiers. This medical facility, however, was particularly reserved for the termi-nally ill. It was said that when a soldier rode the train into that valley, he usually wasn't coming out. They rode the train in to die.

As the war ended, the health spa resumed its original status. Only now it entertained many ex-Confederate soldiers and officers, most notably General Jubal Early. The men would play games, ride horses, and relive the glory days of the war.

Ron Nelson has visited the abandoned resort area to pay homage to the five members of the 17th Virginia Infantry who are buried there. Despite the absence of the impressive rock formation, Ron still felt the hair rise on the back of his neck and head as he walked the valley with his buddy, Bob Fleet.

They walked to the top of the hill where the armchair once stood. Nearby was the marker placed by the U.D.C. in remembrance of the soldiers who died in the hospital. Below them was the single remaining cabin which survived the flash flood. Not far from the lone cabin are the unmarked graves of many a fallen Confederate, sunken plots the only indications of their existence.

Bobby shivered, trying to shake off the sensation of tingling nerves. Even though he was a veteran cop, a place as spooky as Devil's Armchair left an impression on him.

"I have to tell you what happened to me up here about the first trip I made which was in 1988," Bobby began telling his story to Ron. "Tim and I'd been walking around one day. Out of the blue, I became frightened!" Bobby recalled. "There was no logical explanation for it, but I was scared enough that I knew I had to get out of the place!

"We immediately headed for the car. Tim didn't need any explanation, either," Bobby described the scene. "As we drove a few miles down the road, Tim turned to me and said, 'You know, I felt as though a thousand pairs of eyes were watching me back there!'"

Bobby was stunned. He pulled the truck off the road. "That's exactly what I felt and why I wanted to leave!" Bobby declared.

Neither man had 'totally' researched Devil's Armchair previously. After the visit Bob learned that, indeed, one thousand Confederate soldiers died and were buried where they'd walked.

Andersonville Prison

Andersonville, Georgia is a favorite place to visit for people involved in our nation's history. It attracts tourists by the thousands each year. One gentleman in particular was a regular visitor.

Late at night long after the prison was officially closed for the day, Lawrence would make his way into the park. Having spent much of the day imbibing in the local 'brew,' he was ready to sleep it off on one of the park benches. This special occasion was quite memorable for Lawrence.

He woke midst a deep stupor to find several white specters hovering off the ground, getting closer and closer to him. Eerie noises accompanied these movements. Lawrence was terrified.

He ran toward town as fast as his wobbly legs would allow. Quite winded, he began yelling to the townsfolk, "Get up! Get up and come see the spirits out at the old prison!"

A combination of superstition and fear held the people in town for the night. At the advance of daylight, the investigators returned to the scene with him. They walked up Pecan Grove Road to the site of Lawrence's specters. As the group rounded the corner, a herd of forty white-faced goats stared nonchalantly at them. So much for Lawrence's ghosts.

Between February, 1864 and April, 1865, over 40,000 Yankee prisoners of war walked through the gates of Andersonville. Nearly one-third of these men would never again set foot on outside soil.

Its true name was Camp Sumter, but because of its close proximity to Andersonville, the latter became the more popular name.

Prisoners disembarked from the train at the Andersonville Depot and were marched to the prison where they entered the stockade through the North Gate. The stockade enclosed sixteen and a half acres of land and 'housed' 10,000 men in early 1864. By June, 1864 the occupation had grown to 21,000 soldiers. The prison reached its peak of 33,000 in August of that year. Overcrowding, starvation, polluted water and disease took their toll, killing 15,000 prisoners.

As was the case in every Civil War prison, North and South, no one was prepared for the numbers of men who would enter their confines. Nor were they knowledgeable about how to care for them. Nevertheless, Prison Commander Henry Wirz was chosen to atone for these short comings. At the close of the war, Wirz was hung as soldiers around him chanted "Andersonville." With so much anguish, despair and death midst Camp Sumter, it comes as no surprise that some of these energies still linger.

I visited Andersonville April, 1995 where I interviewed volunteers working there. I also spoke with people in the town of Andersonville— people who've spent many years of their lives there. My tape recorder was full of stories regarding the area. What I didn't count on was the extra voice speaking over mine as I faced the Dead House.

There is a tremendous amount of electrical interference on the section of the tape immediately preceding this. Yet, there are no lines or electrical sources midst Andersonville's Dead House area. My own voice is recorded as I spoke about the Pigeon Roost. Then, as though a prisoner from many years ago was standing by my side, a distinct man's voice repeats my words with me! No one was visible near me for several hundred yards!

Mark Stibitz, 1st Corporal of 21st Ohio Volunteer Infantry, Company A, has volunteered his services at Camp Sumter for many years. During one of his evening work periods in 1991 with one of

Nannette Morrison

Reconstructed Shebangs which prisoners 'lived in' at Camp Sumter—April, 1995.

the rangers, the two men experienced audible communication from the Andersonville prisoners.

"It was about dusk when we were working on two different shebangs in the northeastern corner," Mark tells me. "We stopped abruptly and looked at each other. Yet, neither spoke of why he'd paused. So, we continued our construction," Mark said. "We stopped again. This time we asked each other if he'd heard men talking. Both of us agreed that we had. Of course, there was no one else around the acreage." Mark describes the men's voices, "It sounded like a murmur. Words were not distinct. It almost seemed like sounds you'd hear in the distance, only we felt that these were close by us."

In the northwest corner of the cemetery, a gentleman is periodically seen standing outside the brick wall. He leans leisurely against the wall, smoking a pipe, and is dressed in Confederate gray. He wears a greatcoat and a hat. It's usually about dusk when he shows up.

Definitely not from 'modern times,' could this be a Confederate soldier confined in Andersonville long ago?

People residing in the village of Andersonville tell of another sighting. A man traveling on route 49 away from the prison area glanced in the rear view mirror of his car. He saw a soldier run across the road and into the woods. The person he described as seeing fit the description of Wirz as he appeared at the end of the war. The man immediately turned his car around, returning to the location where the apparition had run. Nothing remained to be seen.

Fungstown

John Suchernick, Commander of the 12th Virginia Cavalry (Dismounted), studied for the ministry for several years. Powerful spiritual experiences are not foreign to him. When he visited Fungstown, Maryland, John welcomed his special visitation.

The first year of the Fungstown reenactment event the 12th Virginia Cavalry attended. Most of them knew few details about the skirmish which was a delaying action by Stuart's cavalry and Longstreet's men as they retreated from Gettysburg. This bought decent time for Lee to get across the Potomac River. The fighting was nasty—over six hundred casualties. At one stage the battle was at point-blank range between infantry and artillery. What the 12th Cavalry did not realize until after camp was set up was that they were situated directly on the original Confederate lines.

As soon as John arrived in the camp area, his attention was drawn to a particular outcropping of rocks. For some reason he was fascinated by these rocks. John kept getting the 'impression' that something dramatic had happened there. That feeling persisted throughout the entire event.

The following year the 12th Virginia Cavalry returned to Fungstown for the same event. Again, they were assigned the same area to camp on. John's focus was still drawn to that outcropping of rocks. "I kept thinking, 'there's something there! There has to be something unique about those rocks!'," John recalls. Much later he would learn that a considerable number of soldiers were missing in action. Many were buried all around that area.

The third year of the Fungstown reenactment, John found himself still obsessed with the pile of rocks. At 11:30 p.m. he and his wife took a brief excursion to the latrine which happened to be located fairly close to the outcropping of rocks. While waiting for his wife, John approached the rocks.

A wonderful, peaceful feeling flooded his emotions. Just as this washed over him, a beautiful shaft of light appeared before him. He distinctly received the information that it was the energy of a soldier from long ago. The transparent, whitish form was the size of a person and moved with the pace of one. It walked across the road toward the outcropping of rocks, then disappeared. John's reaction was that of thankfulness, to be privy to such an occurrence singly for his benefit.

He returned to camp but spoke to no one about the experience. This had been a very personal scene he'd witnessed. Somehow, the time wasn't quite right to share it with others. Yet, this fantastic peaceful energy lingered as a reminder for him that 'so many things are possible.'

Johnston's Surrender at Bentonville: Glimpses of 1865

I was in my tent putting some gear away when I heard shouting in the campsite about rebels. Going to investigate, members of my company were walking towards the roadway where a column of Secesh infantry was passing by. These were the element sent to portray Johnston's troops who surrendered to Sherman in North Carolina.

Previously, I thought I would bypass this scenario preferring to eat breakfast and get ready for the afternoon, but something about the rebels intrigued me. Periodically in this hobby, at an event the shrouds of time are pulled back and for an instant, I'll see or feel a moment that coincided with what I so diligently attempt to portray. The demeanor of my Confederate brothers hinted at a glimpse of 1865.

Myself and the other members of my company stood silently watching them pass by, looking splendid with fixed bayonets rhythmically marching to a solemn cadence. Gone was the air of rowdiness which I was accustomed to seeing. They moved silently along but for the drum and the crunching of heavy shoes, many expressionless or solemn at their task. The mounted officers sat very erect, looking very dignified, rarely averting their gaze from the front as they passed.

Prevailing overall was the look of pride about them. They were en route to surrender, but they had meshed with the spirit of their ancestors; the pride of Dixie was alive and well. One could not look upon this collage of butternut and gray without admiration.

After they had passed, a soldier remarked aloud how splendid they looked and that as Union soldiers we should have been assembled to meet them with the respect they deserved. I ran to get my gear as the Union troops were then gathering to move down to the surrender site.

We marched off with fixed bayonets a short distance away to an open field bordered by camera and spectators. As so often happens when we march into the "arena", moments transcend time and space and 1990 became 1865.

Striking me immediately was the heavy silence prevailing over the field, like an event of grave consequences was transpiring. Halting and coming to attention, the air was full of emotion, no one spoke, everyone glancing about for the next activity.

As I marched onto the field, I observed the Confederate standing opposite us. I noticed that the entire line immediately to our front had their backs to us facing another single line of troops a few yards away. Their muskets were already stacked on our arrival, the staffs to the flags lying on top of the stacks.

I was drawn into the scene as it resembled a painting I had seen of Appomattox. The rebels looked peculiar without arms standing across from our ranks, devoid of the accoutrements of war. They stood rigid at attention as their commander met with ours between the lines. Going to parade rest my mind explored the sensations, thoughts and emotions that I beheld.

I began to feel sad for the Confederate troops empathizing my own feelings as a surrendering Southern soldier. Most of the battle flags had been pulled off the staffs, shredded and distributed amongst the troops as they were at the end of the war. I could envision looking at the staff and remembering the banner flying defiantly over the countless battlefields where untold numbers of beloved comrades had perished.

Now all that remained would be a tattered remnant stored for posterity in a family Bible, a picture frame or storage chest. As the years would go by the veteran would tell of the days when he marched with Lee, Johnston or Longstreet and this little bit of cloth would be brought out in testimony for admiring generations to see. However, now he saw the stark reality of the barren staff knowing all the blood that had been spilled in its behalf. He had seen the ashen faces, the lifeless bodies, desperate fighting, endless marching, sleepless nights, days without food, the homeland burned and now surrender.

The Southern commander barked out the order to dismiss and they began to break ranks and move away. A Southern officer drawled, "Go on home," breaking the silence, eliciting a command all had hoped for years would be possible.

With dejected, somber faces they shuffled off the field away from their stacked muskets and our formation, glancing at each other as they went. Perhaps they wondered in disbelief that the war was really over for them, if their homes would be there when they arrived, if anyone would be there to greet them or what the uncertain future would hold.

As we stood in silence watching them walk away from us, I felt sad as a reenactor seeing this as my last 125th anniversary battle. I thought back to those large scale events that let me touch my heritage through all my senses, exceeding the limits of imagination while reading a book.

Gone was Gettysburg, the likes of which I'll never see again in my lifetime. I can still see the thousands of troops in formation, feel the air crackle with electrical sensation of anticipation of battle at McPhersons Ridge, or dashing across the wheat field to the cheers of hundreds of troops attempting to save the Union right. I thought of Picketts' charge the grandest spectacle of all, and the spontaneous silent tribute to their sacrifice thereafter, so overwhelming that I am sure their spirits walked among us. I had seen the intensity of battle in the wilderness, dawn attack at the Mule Shoe, and the futile charges at Atlanta.

Portraying a Union soldier at the surrender I felt vastly relieved. Long gone was the glorious revelry of war. The last few years had come down to the lowly private, devoted to duty, seeing the job done regardless of the sacrifice. He too had seen his share of hardship, death and deprivation, was desperately tired of it all and only wanted to go home. He carried memories of wasted lives in futile assaults against impregnable positions and lost opportunities in poor leadership. But now all that was behind him, it was over.

The Confederates stopped at the edge of the field at a wood line and gathered in groups. As it was Sunday morning, many knelt in final prayer together as I am sure they did then, a last fellowship with their comrades. A lone bagpiper and drummer in their ranks began to play "Amazing Grace." At that we uncovered in respect to their ceremony. The Confederate commander, with reins in hand knelt beside his horse. The piper finished "Amazing Grace" and as the drum rolled, played "Dixie," a slow measured chorus in the spirit of the moment. At the conclusion, we watched as the groups stayed together for speeches or prayers by the officers symbolic of the last gatherings before they started their journey home. One by one, the ceremonies concluded and the groups began to disperse. The memory of the scene I will carry with me, the final act of a niche in time so long ago.

Written around April, 1990 by Larry Jones

A Cry for Help

Dear Ms. Morrison:

I was so glad that I found your writing in the Indiana, Pennsylvania Paper about the things that are happening at Gettysburg, and it just seemed that you hit right on the button for me. You see, my husband and I were down there this spring and we could only stay for a day and a half and I had to leave. When we first got there I sensed more unleashed energy and unrest than I could handle. We walked on the hills and took the tours around Gettysburg and I actually couldn't hardly stand it, the tension was so high in me. We stopped at a memorial and we walked up and down the steps and the thousands of names that were on it was mind boggling. I was very tense and upset most of the time. I went up to a name and put my fingers on the name and all of a sudden I felt like someone had hit me in the chest with something, I lost my breath and staggered back, the panic that I felt was terrible like a panic for my very life. Much to say I didn't do that again.

But that night was the worst, we were in this nice hotel in town. It was below a big hill where many men had been killed. I couldn't sleep, I tossed and turned and finally I fell asleep. I couldn't stay asleep because in my dreams all I saw was this short, very black tunnel, but at the other end of the tunnel was all these men's faces, pushing into my sight like they were trying to see me and talk to me. I was terrified. They kept pushing each other back so the other one could talk. I couldn't hear their voices but I could see their lips

134

moving. I could see the pain on their faces. The last one that I saw I could read his lips and he was saying, "Help me."

I woke up and was so upset, I sat up for a while and I looked out the window. I paced the room and finally at around 4 a.m. I was so tired that I decided to lie down again. Again I had the same dreams of someone trying to get in contact with me.

I'm not a psychic, but I've had lots of experiences and I absolutely do not try to encourage them. They scare me very badly. I am a Christian and I do not believe that I should pursue this any further. But I am so glad to have someone to tell this to. This lifts a weight off my shoulders to tell someone who will understand.

The next day we were driving around and I saw this man dressed in old clothes and a floppy old hat, ragged pants, and dirty old shoes. He was walking along the road. I had the weirdest feeling about him. No one else was around. He turned and looked straight at me. It seemed that he looked inside my eyes to my soul.

When we first got there I wanted to stay in this house really bad down town. I was obsessed with staying there, but there weren't any rooms left. Later at the museum I bought a tape about the hauntings of Gettysburg. That house was on the list as one of the most haunted ones there. There is definitely something in Gettysburg that will never leave. They are begging for someone to get their stories out; I feel that they are trapped there and can't get home. I feel better talking to you about this.

Thank you again,

A.F.B.

Afterword

Through my efforts writing *A Thundering Silence* and *Echoes of Valor*, I have come to learn far more about the spiritual realms. I now have a greater respect for the capabilities of the energy forms among us.

My thanks and encouragement go out to the hundreds of people contacting me with their versions of spirits at unrest. These spiritual people are sincere about understanding the transformation of energy, as well as assisting those which are 'soul complexes remaining in confusion.'

The support of countless fellow voyagers is appreciated in assembling *A Thundering Silence*: Hook (yet in the service 'unofficially' of our federal government), Bob Talbot, Jane M. Lawson, George Leeper, Larry Jones, Charles Spicer, Michael Smith, Frank Loughran, Linda Timberlake, and Michele Gray for typing on such a sensitive manuscript.

For further contacts on specific areas and work, addresses are offered:

Martha Washington Inn
150 West Main Street
Abingdon, VA 24210
(800) 533-1014

Meadow Farm
P.O. Box 27032
Richmond, VA 23273
(804) 672-5106

Jackson's Mill State 4-H Conference Center
P.O. Box 670
Weston, WV   26452
(304) 269-5100

Kenmore Mansion
1201 Washington Ave.
Fredericksburg, VA   22401
(703) 373-3381

Olustee Battlefield State Historic Site
P.O. Box 40
Olustee, FL   32072
(904) 758-0400

Andersonville Prison State Park
Andersonville, GA

Droop Mountain State Park
   HC64, Box 189
   Hillsboro, W.VA 24946

Nannette Morrison
c/o Encore Effects
1310 Lester Drive
Charlottesville, VA   22901
(804) 293-9650

For further reading on this subject, Mark Nesbitt's *Gettysburg Ghosts* I and II offer similar accounts. Mark's third book on ghosts of Gettysburg will be available soon. Thomas Publications, P.O. Box 3031, Gettysburg, PA 17325 has copies. *Echoes of Valor*, my first book on these areas, is available by writing to me.

References

Chaitin, Peter M., and Time-Life Books Editors *The Coastal War-Chesapeake Bay to Rio Grande.* Alexandria, Va: Time-Life Books, 1984.

Evans-Wentz, W.Y., Editor *The Tibetan Book of the Dead.* London, England: Oxford University Press, 1960.

Furgurson, Ernest B. *Chancellorsville 1863.* New York, NY: Alfred A. Knopf, 1992.

Godwin, Malcolm *Angels, An Endangered Species.* New York, NY: Simon and Schuster, 1990.

Gluckman, Col. Arcadi *Identifying Old U.S. Muskets, Rifles and Carbines.* New York, NY: Bonanza Books, 1959.

Johnson, Echols and Willis, Brenda L. *Hard Times 1861-1865,* Vol. 1.